LOS ANGELES
"THE MAGIC CITY"

ICONIC
LA

ICONIC LA

Stories of LA's Most Memorable Buildings

Gloria Koenig

Foreword by
Frank O. Gehry

Published in the United States of America 2000

Design by Jim Drobka
Edited by Danette Riddle
Imaging and production by Navigator Press, Pasadena, California
Printed in Hong Kong

For information address
Balcony Press
512 E. Wilson Suite 306
Glendale, California 91206

ICONIC L.A. ©2000 Gloria Koenig

Library of Congress Catalog Card Number: 00-131710
ISBN 1-890449-08-3

I dedicate this book to my husband,
Pierre Koenig, whose inspiring work was its genesis.

CONTENTS

ICONIC L.A. is a chronicle of a city in progress, an urban biography that tells a century's worth of history through the profiles of the thirteen buildings in the book. Combined, they form a fusion of architecture, from the San Fernando Rey Mission deep in the Valley to my Disney Concert Hall in the heart of Downtown Los Angeles, that pretty much represents what has gone on here in the last one hundred years. Climate, open land and the lack of entrenched social-political traditions have contributed to the potential for innovation and invention in this land sometimes called Eden.

This is a city of instant recognition, a collection of images disseminated by photographs and films that people have come to envision as laid-back Los Angeles, the place where movies are made and trends are tried out. For me, L.A. has always offered a kind of freewheeling chaotic order, built around the automobile and the ultimate icon of its massive freeway system.

I'm intrigued by its strengths and weaknesses and see Los Angeles as a manifestation of our time. It's a city of diversity, from its demographics to its politics to its architecture, and it has evolved from an arid pueblo in the middle of nowhere to a major metropolis that has become one of the most famous cities in the world.

My family came to Los Angeles from Toronto, Canada, when I was sixteen. I worked here, went to school at the University of Southern California here; and, after a year in Paris, started my practice here in Brentwood and then on the oceanfront at Venice Beach. During those years of the early '60s, no one expected significant architecture to come out of L.A. Critics dismissed the city as kind of interesting but basically unimportant which allowed a lot of room for artistic experimentation and freedom. Historically,

Los Angeles has always been open to suggestion from all of the art forms, promoting experimentation and allowing the intuitive response to the landscape and the weather that has created the range of architecture portrayed in ICONIC L.A.

The individual buildings examined here, each with its own distinguishing characteristics, are recognized throughout the world, but when grouped together under one umbrella, they demonstrate the singular power and personality of Los Angeles as a major metropolis. Not all of them were welcomed when first proposed, but the passage of time has allowed their images to become firmly imprinted in the minds of people around the globe. The buildings are very different from one another, but all represent a break through for their given time in history and still stand out as icons today. Sooner or later, good art and good architecture emerge from the ongoing evolutionary cycle. ICONIC L.A. is an historic preservation of these buildings in the form of prose that offers a composite image of some of the city's outstanding architectural achievements.

Frank O. Gehry

Fokker Tri-motor Airplane over City Hall, c. 1929

INTRODUCTION

Shortly after the turn of the century, Los Angeles began its lazy sprawl across the western edge of the continent, a laid-back, sundrenched town shaped by orange groves and movie shoots, inventing itself as it went along. Unsure of its destination but exuberant about getting there, the city came along at a seminal moment in the country's history—an intersection of time and space that would lead to the singular and thriving metropolis it has become. According to historian Reyner Banham, Los Angeles has the most creative architectural history of any city in the United States, and its landmarks reflect the exhilarating heterogeneity of its built environment.

Known by the lengthy name *El Pueblo de Nuestra Señora la Reina de Los Angeles*, Los Angeles began as four square leagues of land somewhere in the vicinity of the Plaza Church and the Olvera Street complex. The actual site of the original settlement plaza is unknown, as the early pueblo was moved several times in response to flooding and earthquakes. The Downtown area around the townsite developed randomly, and Greater Los Angeles began to take actual shape with the coming of the railroads, which built the first lines from the pueblo outward toward the burgeoning regions of San Fernando Valley, Santa Monica, San Bernardino, Anaheim and Wilmington. The chronology of the city's past can be traced along these railway lines and along the freeways that followed their path.

Throughout the 20th century, Los Angeles has not paused in its exponential growth despite earthquakes, floods and fires, economic booms and busts and recurrent social upheavals that have marked its passage. From early mission days as Pueblo Los Angeles, to its current status as one of the world's great cities, it has contributed more than its share of great art and celebrated artists to the planet. Polemicists dismiss Los Angeles as "La La Land," yet the city has ineluctably shown itself to be a center of enormous cultural innovation and accomplishment.

The vigorous mix of buildings that spread across the greater Los Angeles landscape form an architectural web that is eclectic—not in the pejorative sense, but as a multiform manifestation of free and uninhibited growth. This has always been a city of "anything goes," a place that has sanctioned the shifting seasons of style in domestic and commercial architecture that result in today's richly divergent communities.

The thirteen buildings in this book frame the evolution of these differences, beginning with the Spanish colonial Mission San Fernando Rey de España and ending with the undulating sculptural surfaces of the Disney Concert Hall. In between are representations of the Mission Style, Spanish Colonial Revival, Beaux Arts, Pre-Columbian, Mayan, Modern, Post-Modern and High Tech. Each segment is a transitional time capsule containing within it the artifacts of the building's history, including visual mementos such as blueprints, drawings, scale models and sequential construction photographs. The delicate balance between the client, the architect and the land, always a dramatic component of any architectural project, is investigated and discussed whenever the historical facts are available. Present-day use and future plans complete the descriptions. Combined, these landmark structures form a montage of architecture that is hard-wired in the collective memory as the composite iconic image of Los Angeles.

MISSION SAN FERNANDO REY DE ESPAÑA

The twenty-one missions, from San Diego in the South to Sonoma in the North, are icons that recall the settling of 'Alta California' and the psychological and spiritual link that once connected the disparate towns along the coast.

The replica bell markers stationed intermittently along U.S. Highway 101 are nostalgic reminders of another culture and another time when the Missions dominated the architectural landscape of provincial *Alta California*. The highway was once a part of the network of indigenous trails the Indians traveled to get from village to village, later becoming a foot path for the *Padres*— a rustic narrow track that connected the growing chain of missions along the Pacific Coast from San Diego Alcala in the south, to San Francisco Solano at Sonoma in the north. The 500 mile long trail was called *El Camino Real*, the Royal Road, in honor of the Spanish Crown.

As rulers of half of the New World in the late 1700s, Spain was skilled at "planting" settlements, having successfully done so for two hundred years as they acquired the frontier outposts of their far-flung empire. The colonization of California was to have been accomplished efficiently, using a

Early agrarian days at the Mission

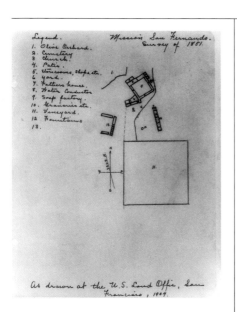

TOP LEFT   *Original sketches of the Mission floor plans, c. 1851*

LEFT   *Exposed* Padrillo *bricks*

ABOVE   *The twenty-one arches of the Convento colonnade*

"Then came the Padres to California...They built simply, strongly, but...with as much beauty as possible. The style was a variety of Spanish-Colonial of Mexico, but really it was a new style–the Mission style of California."
SANTA BARBARA NEWS PRESS, August 18, 1932

stringent set of prearranged rules, "The Laws of the Indies," a civil code that served as a blueprint covering all the contingencies that their experience had taught them could occur. Nothing was left to chance; there was paperwork for everything. The Padres were sent forth with a military escort to establish missions that would stake out the territory, to cultivate the land with crops and livestock, and to proselytize Christianity to the indigenous population. The plan stated that mission lands would be held in trust for the Indian neophytes for ten years, subsequently becoming the center of their towns and pueblos.

The Shoshone Indians called it *Achois Camihabit,* the lush and humid land in the spacious valley that was the site of an ancestral village. It was fed by four running streams, had abundant supplies of stone and limestone, and was ideal for agricultural development, attributes eminently suitable for establishing the mission between San Gabriel and San Buenaventura. The location chosen in the valley was the Reyes Rancho, a provisional grant of land made by the Governor to Don Francisco Reyes, Alcalde of the Pueblo of Los Angeles. After a short scuffle, Reyes gave up his land when he realized it was legally owned by Mission San Gabriel. On September 8, 1797, Father Fermin de Lasuen, successor to Father Junipero Serra, assisted by resident missionaries, Fray Francisco Dumetz and Fray Juan Cortez, conducted opening ceremonies to inaugurate Mission San Fernando Rey de España.

All of the missions conformed to the basic pattern established in the monasteries built by Conquistadors in Mexico: a large quadrangle of buildings constructed in the semi-Moorish style of architecture prevalent in the Spanish provinces, built around an open center courtyard with the church situated at a corner. San Fernando Rey was planned in the requisite manner, developing a characteristic style that was determined by what the land could offer in the way of building materials, and by what the Padres, with their subliminal echoes of remembered Spanish, Moorish and Mexican architecture, could offer in the way of building

design. No construction plans or drawings from this period exist today, though most structures appear to have been built as needed with the Padre as client and whatever artisan he could find as contractor. Although an occasional designer or engineer came from Mexico to work with the missionaries, the natural skill and craftsmanship of the local Shoshone Indians combined with the inventive tutelage of the Padres, contributed greatly to the ongoing construction process.

The basic building block of the mission was the *padrillo,* the adobe brick used to construct almost everything, from inner and outer walls and floors, to the buttresses and piers that helped to hold them in place. The adobe was a concoction of earth, clay, sand, straw, chaff, and sometimes tiny fragments of tile and stone. It was mixed with water to the desired consistency and then shaped in wooden molds and put out in the sun to dry. The size of the molds depended on the use of the brick and ranged from square, flat floor tiles to the massive adobe blocks that faced the outside of the structures. These were plastered over with a lime and sand mixture to protect the porous adobe, as did the sloping overhangs of red clay roof tiles that were eventually built to shield the walls from the weather. The ubiquitous terra cotta tiles, or *tejas,* were molded in hollowed-out forms that shaped them into 22-inch lengths, 9 inches wide at the top and tapering to 5 inches at the bottom. The fan-shaped tile accommodated the overlay process on the roofs. An early form of air-conditioning was devised by elevating the tiles on willow poles that were lain across wooden beams, allowing cool air to circulate beneath them. The foundations for all the adobe structures were shallow trenches dug out and filled with rocks and stones from the nearby streams.

Miraculously, it was only two months after the inauguration of San Fernando Rey that its first adobe church was completed and ready for services. A temporary edifice, the small chapel was used for only two years when a larger church was built for the growing congregation. It in turn was replaced in another two years when a permanent church was dedicated on December 6, 1806. This rectangular building was 185 feet long and 35 feet wide, the width determined by the availability of the roofing beams hewn from the standing timber hauled in from the Sierra Madre foothills. The walls, which were constructed on a tapering angle and appeared to be pitched outward, were five feet thick at the base, decreasing to three feet thick at the top. Near the sacristy were two massive buttresses strengthening the walls which were divided into separate panels by eight structural pilasters. On the patio side of the chapel, a two-story bell tower with three arched openings housed the mission's three bells, and a choir loft on the second level reached via an adobe stairway. This third chapel survived the vicissitudes of California earthquake and weather until the 1971 temblor reduced it to rubble. An historically accurate replica, complete with the original mission bells, was created on its site.

Within this time period, the mission grew into a thriving community, a self-sufficient village with housing built for nearly a thousand neophytes. The original quadrangle was 295 by 315 feet when completed, and was edged with kitchens, a grist mill, dormitories, barracks, workshops, storerooms, a tannery, carpenter shop and granaries that formed a small walled city. A tract of about 15 square miles surrounding the mission complex was used for agriculture and cattle-raising. Field crops of wheat, barley, corn, and peas, as well as lush groves of olive, fruit, nut and date trees were successfully cultivated on the fertile and irrigated land, supplying not only the mission's growing population, but the people of the nearby Pueblo de Los Angeles as well.

Around 1806, work began on what was to become one of the most preeminent structures of the entire mission system and the largest adobe building in all of California. The Convento, or fathers' dwelling, was built, according to evidence revealed in subsequent earthquakes, in several phases over a period of years and was completed in 1822 when a wall was constructed to enclose its adjoining courtyard. The finished building, with adobe walls four feet thick, was 243 feet in length by 50 feet wide and at the apex of the ceiling it rose to 45 feet in height. The interior contained over 20 rooms, including a chapel, resident priest's quarters, guest accommodations, a library, a refectory, a large reception room or *sala,* a kitchen, a long storeroom and a ramp leading down to a wine cellar. But it is the exterior of the majestic Convento with its long colonnade of Roman style arches, nineteen across the front and one at each end, that remains to haunt the nostalgic memory of each passing generation of visitors to San Fernando Mission. Extending across the entire south end of the monastery building, the arched promenade is paved with adobe tile and topped at the west end with a small bell tower made of *padrillos* and mortar. Although the building originally had a flat roof with terra cotta drain pipes, it was covered over around 1812 with a two-sloped tile roof that enclosed the Convento's massive proportions in classic mission style architecture.

The process called secularization took a terrible toll on the California missions. It began in 1810 with the *Grito de Independencia,* The Cry for Independence, when the Republic of Mexico broke away from Spain and supplies and funds were abruptly cut off, leaving the missions in a state of anarchy and confusion. As early as 1813, orders were issued to turn the missions over to civilian authority, and the Padres waged a desperate battle to keep the status quo. In 1833, the confiscation process began in earnest, and the mission system began to disintegrate. The plan was to evolve the properties from missions into pueblos under civilian authority, where each Indian family was to live and cultivate their own assigned plots of land. However, they were ill-prepared for the sudden responsibility, and most lost their land or were cheated out of it by speculators within a few months of receiving it. Drastic changes on the mission lands continued, with raw materials and herds of livestock divided, and crops often abandoned and left to die. The new instant pueblos did not last long and the quadrangle at San Fernando Rey, which was secularized in 1834, was soon deserted. Many of the buildings were vandalized for timber, roof tiles, window glass and hardware, leaving them exposed to the elements and weakened and vulnerable to earthquakes. This depreda-

TOP   *Present day Mission courtyard*

ABOVE   *Historically accurate replica of the first Mission church*

"The conviction comes strong on one that in no civilized country in the world save our own, would such despoliation grow unhindered—with no hand to stay it. No Californian can view these picturesque ruins and fail to become an enthusiastic advocate of mission restoration."

Joseph R. Knowland, President, California Historic Landmarks League

tion continued until the American occupation of California, when the Federal Land Commission began a review of property rights. By the time President Abraham Lincoln signed the agreement in 1861 that returned part of the original mission compound to the Franciscan Order, it was almost too late for retrieval.

The Convento had managed to survive throughout this degenerative period because of the series of lessees that lived there over the decades keeping the building habitable, including U.S. Army Colonel John Fremont and his troops, Andres Pico, the Butterfield Stage Line and George K. Porter, who acquired the land surrounding the mission and used the Convento as headquarters for the Porter Land and Water Company. However, by 1896, the historic structure was being used as a hog farm and the Landmarks Club, a group of concerned citizens determined to restore the California missions, raised enough money to repair the mission church as well as the roof and walls of the Convento in time for the mission's 1897 Centennial.

Founded by Los Angeles journalist Charles Fletcher Lummis, the Landmarks Club pioneered the restoration of the missions in Southern California, saving many of them from total ruin. The members were early conservationists who campaigned vigorously for funds to undertake the renovations and repairs necessary to bring the missions back to life. By 1916, when the Convento's roof had blown off in a storm and the building was once again badly in need of restoration, the Landmarks Club organized a fundraising event called "Candle Day," a unique festivity that drew a crowd of six thousand people to the mission grounds. The candles were sold at a dollar each, and when darkness fell, the donors lit them simultaneously and walked together through the Convento's arched colonnade. The dedicated group continued its efforts to preserve the missions as significant historic buildings and was instrumental in preserving the legacy of Mission San Fernando Rey.

Today the Mission, a registered state monument, is an oasis of serenity in the midst of the busy San Fernando Valley.

OPPOSITE *Restored Mission church interior*
ABOVE *The Mission after secularization in 1834*

The Convento has been earthquake retrofitted with steel reinforcements and all of its floors, walls and ceilings have been refinished. A thirty-five bell carillon has been installed in the bell tower of the replica chapel along with the original mission bells. The parking area has been resurfaced and an aggregate walkway guides visitors, over 100,000 a year, around the extensive gardens. An Archival Center and Historical Museum are available to the public three days a week. A favorite field trip for Los Angeles area school children, Mission San Fernando Rey allows them to experience their heritage firsthand, to feel what it was like to walk through the Convento's arcade two hundred years ago, when the freeways were foot trails and the pastoral land of the San Fernando Valley stretched limitlessly, as far as the eye could see.

THE BRADBURY BUILDING

The indelible image of the Bradbury Building in the 1982 film Bladerunner, evoked the sense of what it was originally: a building of the future designed from the past.

"A vast hall full of light, received not alone from the windows on all sides but from the dome, the point of which was a hundred feet above...The walls were frescoed in mellow tints, to soften without absorbing the light which flooded the interior."
LOOKING BACKWARD, **EDWARD BELLAMY**

This quote, from an 1887 science fiction novel describing the author's vision of a commercial building in the 21st century, had a profound effect on George Herbert Wyman, designer of the Bradbury Building. It is ironic that the building would then become world famous as the symbol of futuristic Los Angeles in the 1982 Ridley Scott film, *Bladerunner*.

A draftsman in the Dayton, Ohio office of his uncle, Luther Peters, Wyman moved to Los Angeles with the firm Peters and Burns, when they received the commission to

The Bradbury's incognito exterior

design some of the early buildings at the Sawtelle National Military Home. After a few years, the partnership of Peters and Burns was dissolved, and when Luther Peters moved on to build several downtown office buildings with architect Sumner P. Hunt, his nephew also went to work in Hunt's Los Angeles office. It was here that Lewis Bradbury discovered the young draftsman, and chose him over principal architect Hunt to design the commercial building he hoped would bring him immortality.

The contrast of the incognito exterior of the Bradbury Building with its brilliant interior is certainly one of its most dramatic aspects, a play of forces that somehow creates its own powerful synergy. The exterior facade of brick masonry with sandstone trim is accented with arched clerestory windows along the upper story and a row of commercial shops at ground level—all of it adding up to a blandly conservative version of the Romanesque Revival architecture so common to business districts in the last years of the 19th Century. The entrance at Broadway and Third leads into a foyer with still no hint of what is to come until a few steps later when the interior opens up into an atrium that is a soaring prism of light, the rectilinear space of the narrow 50 by 120-foot courtyard widening as it rises exponentially to the pitched glass canopy five stories overhead. This glazed skylight is made of iron webbing filled with elongated rectangles of opapue glass that allow the weather to become a daily part of life within the building. Supporting the ceiling elements are ironwork trusses that seem to float just below the clerestory windows, their perfectly proportioned scrollwork corners an elegant and masterful engineering achievement.

Two wrought-iron staircases with treads of Italian rose marble that slide into openwork metal strings, rise at opposite ends of the ground floor. Art Nouveau balustrades of wood and cast iron enclose the second, third and fourth floor balconies which are supported by Corinthian columns on all four sides of the light-filled center court. At the north and south sides of the building, the famous open cage elevators with their clicking hyraulic mechanisms and free-standing grillwork shafts, glide up and down with their moving counter-weights in view. The offices are spacious and comfortable with 12 to 14-foot high ceilings, carved red oak wainscoting and fascias, and windowsills of rose-colored marble. An inlay of this marble is used as a baseboard outlining all of the tile floors on each level of the building, creating a color palette of glowing tones that integrates the many disparate details of the building's intricate and bold design into a unified whole.

Lewis Bradbury was a real estate tycoon who made his fortune in the Mazatlan gold mines of Mexico. In 1892, the same year that he began construction on his famous building, he established a town named Bradbury, buying up 2,750 acres of ranch land where he built his own hacienda. Bordered by Duarte, Monrovia and the Angeles National Forest, 23 miles northeast of Los Angeles, the community was called "The City of Rural Tranquillity." At this time, Bradbury was aging and in failing health, and he wanted to create a building that would be a monument to his life; a structure that would reflect his vision of himself and his impact on the city of Los Angeles. He bought a block of land in the growing business district of the downtown area, a short walk from the 50-room Victorian mansion he had built for himself and his family on Bunker Hill. He commissioned architect Sumner P. Hunt to design a five-story office building for the site at the southwest corner of Broadway and Third.

Hunt's drawings did not begin to approximate what Bradbury had in mind. They were too staid and conventional and when communication between the two men broke down, Hunt relinquished the work to George Wyman who was deeply involved in the preliminary planning stages of the building and had been revising Hunt's drawings to accommodate Bradbury's changes. An unproven 32-year old with no professional education in architecture or engineering, Wyman's unorthodox concepts seemed to mesh with what Bradbury had been trying to convey in his unformed but visionary ideas. While traveling in Europe the developer

CURRIER BLOCK AND BRADBURY BUILDING, CORNER OF BROADWAY AND THIRD STREET.

LEONARD MERRILL,
(Real Estate, R. 240-241)
Bradbury Building

BROUSSEAU & MONTGOMERY,
Attorneys at Law, R. 403)

H. BERT ELLIS, M.D.
(Room 243)

GEO. H. WYMAN
(Architect of Bradbury Building)
Rooms 305-307

S. S. SALISBURY, M.D.
(Room 234)

CHARLES UDELL,
(Attorney at Law and Notary
Public, Suite 401)

DR. HERBERT D. REQUA,
(Dentist, Room 418)
F. F. BICKNELL, M.D.

DR. H. C. BUELL,
(Dentist, R. 218-219)
A. L. MOORE, M.D.

TOP   *Vintage rendering of the Bradbury's exterior*
MIDDLE   *American Institute of Architects Offices, 1969*
ABOVE   *Roof view of glazed skylight and clerestory windows*
RIGHT   *Restoration of individual glass panels*

ABOVE   *Exposed iron balustrades frame stairwells and corridors*
RIGHT   *Hydraulic birdcage elevators are located at each end of the courtyard.*

had seen Eiffel's 1876 Bon Marche Department Store and Labrouste's 1858 Bibliotheque Nationale, buildings of the Cast Iron Age with exposed iron stairways and glazed roofs. George Wyman's perception of futuristic buildings with crystal courts was straight out of the current cult science fiction novel he had been reading. Because the two men were a subliminal match, they were able to work together easily, each understanding the other's ideas with a kind of mental shorthand.

However, when it came down to actually taking over the job, Wyman was reluctant to accept the commission. He was all too aware of his lack of training, and although the prospect of designing a building on his own was exhilarating, it also filled him with dread. At this point, according to Wyman's daughter, a "Ouija" board made the decision for him. A young man with a distinctly mystical outlook on life, he consulted what was then called a "Planchette" which told him in no uncertain terms, "Take the Bradbury. It will make you famous." Inexplicably, the word "Bradbury" was written upside down, but the message was clearly legible and for Wyman, the problem was solved and the decision was made. He began work on the building that over the years has proved the Ouija board's prediction to be weirdly accurate because it did, indeed, make Wyman famous.

When construction began in 1892, a major problem was unearthed when they began to excavate for the foundation. A vigorous artesian spring was discovered on the site. Prior to 1899, Los Angeles had no building codes to set the standards for construction, yet Bradbury and Wyman realized the running water could eventually undermine their structure. In spite of the considerable expense, they opted for maximum safety and strengthened the foundation with massive steel beams imported from Europe. Demonstrating the characteristic ingenuity used throughout the construction phase, Wyman turned a bad thing into a good thing, utilizing the energy of the active spring to supply steam for the building and to run the two hydraulic elevators. But the ground water and other problems inherent in building a structure so unique for its time caused construction costs to double, soaring from an estimate of $250,000 to $500,000, an extravagant amount of money for the era. Overseeing the entire construction process were Bradbury's attorneys, John Bicknell and Walter Trask, partners in the firm that was to become Gibson, Dunn & Crutcher. They became the building's first tenants.

In spite of the many obstacles along the way, the building was completed in 1893, only a year after construction began, but not soon enough for Lewis Bradbury, who died a few months before the opening ceremonies without seeing his completed masterpiece. George Wyman went on to

RIGHT   *Light-filled span of the Bradbury's interior*
ABOVE   *The Iron mail drop was innovative for its time.*

enroll in a correspondence course in architecture to better learn the rules of the game and then designed several Los Angeles buildings, including the Ferguson Building at the foot of Angel's Flight; the Tahoe Building for Bradbury's son; and a remodel of the Jonathan Club. But the Bradbury was the single extraordinary achievement of his lifetime, and the one for which he is remembered.

In September of 1962, the Bradbury Building was named an Historic Cultural Monument by the Los Angeles Cultural Heritage Board, and it also received federal recognition when it was added to the National Register of Historic Structures. The building fell on hard times during the 1940s when several of the upper loft spaces were used as sewing

rooms for garment factories, reflecting the fact that at one time, the Broadway district was the garment manufacturing capitol of the Los Angeles wholesale trade. In 1969, the Bradbury underwent a major restoration that reclaimed it from long years of neglect and decay, but after the 1971 earthquake, it needed extensive retrofitting to meet the stringent standards of the city's new building codes. A very extensive and costly seismic renovation was undertaken and finally completed at a cost of 2.4 million dollars.

In 1989, downtown Los Angeles developer Ira Yellin bought the landmark building with the intention of revitalizing the aging Broadway and Third Street neighborhood where he already owned the Million Dollar Theater and Grand Central Market across the street from the Bradbury. Comparing his parcel of historic buildings to successful redevelopments such as Harbor Place and Faneuil Hall in Boston, Yellin's goal was to create a vital link between the Civic Center to the north, Bunker Hill to the west, Little Tokyo to the east, and the downtown retail district to the south. A partnership headed by Yellin's company began a painstaking process of renovation under the direction of restoration architect Brenda A. Levin, who had to maintain a precarious balance between preserving every architectural detail of the historic building while modernizing it to meet current office standards and the necessary safety codes mandated by the city. One of many agonizing decisions concerned the Bradbury's famous skylight which contained more than 50 panes of broken untempered glass. The choice was between replacing the whole skylight, with tempered glass or keeping the existing glass with wire mesh below. Because the new panels could have changed the amazing quality of the light in the atrium, Levin decided to keep the original glass, a judgement typical of the responsible supervision used throughout the preservation procedure. The finished building has 61,000 square feet of office space on the top four floors and 17,000 square feet of retail space on the ground floor level.

The Hollyhock House was the precursor to the famous Frank Lloyd Wright textile block houses, set high on a hill in Hollywood among a grove of olive trees. As Wright himself said, "The land is the beginning of architecture."

FRANK LLOYD WRIGHT

REMEMBERED, John H. Howe

There is an intangible quality of light in old photographs of Southern California, gradients of color that seep through the black and white surface and viscerally inform the viewer of another time. Hollywood in 1919, the year that Aline Barnsdall purchased land on which to build an artistic commune, appears to have been drenched in that light, a city full of promise and wide-open possibility. Here, the oil heiress had found the setting for her dream of a community dedicated to the theatrical arts.

Set into the beautiful landscape of the hills and mountains beyond, Barnsdall's property was a 36-acre olive orchard that rose to a gentle slope one hundred feet above the level streets of small one-story bungalows below. Olive Hill was encircled by a rising geometric grid of 1,154 olive trees that stopped short of the summit, leaving a flat pad of buildable land with a 360-degree panoramic view. Off in the distance

The hollyhock theme was reiterated throughout the interior spaces.

TOP   *Olive Hill was encircled by a rising geometric grid of 1,154 olive trees.*

LEFT   *Frank Lloyd Wright*

ABOVE   *Aline Barnsdall*

*"A restless spirit - disinclined to stay long at any time
in any one place as she traveled over the face of the globe,
she would drop suggestions as a war-plane drops bombs
and sail away into the blue. One never knew when or
from where the bombs would drop - but they dropped."*
AN AUTOBIOGRAPHY, Frank Lloyd Wright

were wide swaths of agricultural land and beyond that, the blue expanse of the Pacific Ocean. The parcel was almost the size of a quarter section, a square plot of rural land bounded by Hollywood Boulevard on the north; Sunset Boulevard on the south; Edgemont Street on the west and Vermont Avenue on the east. Entrances to the property were at the northeast and southeast corners, and winding access roads curved gently through the groves of 30-year old trees converging at the crest.

Olive Hill was once part of the vast 6,647-acre rancho granted to Josef Vicente Feliz in 1802. Not far from the original Pueblo De Los Angeles, the historic acreage was often the site of Easter Sunrise Services and seemed a likely place for a public park. The parcel had been for sale by a widow named Mary Harrison Spires for several years at an asking price of $360,000, or $10,000 dollars an acre. Aline Barnsdall offered $300,000 dollars in cash for the 36 acres and it was accepted. She was very rich, very dedicated to the arts, and very determined to make a lasting contribution to culture; all she needed now was her architect.

Barnsdall had met Frank Lloyd Wright towards the end of 1914 when she was producing experimental plays at a rented 99-seat theater in the Fine Arts Building in Chicago. She greatly admired Wright's Midway Gardens, an entertainment complex that combined a restaurant, cafe and beer garden with concordant landscaping, that had been recently completed in Washington Park. Introduced to Wright by Henry Blackman Sell, literary editor for the Chicago Daily News, Barnsdall wanted the progressive architect to design a multi-story theater for her production group, the Players Producing Company, and for The Chicago Little Theater. She envisioned a building that housed a theater at its center surrounded by actor's and musician's studios to provide rental income so that the building could pay for itself while supporting her artistic endeavors. Although she was a wealthy heiress, she was always a cautious businesswoman and tried to protect her investments.

Louise Aline Barnsdall was born on April 1, 1882. in Pittsburgh, Pennsylvania. Her grandfather, William Barnsdall, was an immigrant shoemaker from England who successfully drilled for oil and then built the country's first oil refinery, making millions in the process. Her father, Theodore Newton Barnsdall, drilled his own oil well when he was sixteen years old and branched out into mining gold and silver as well as coal, iron and zinc. The family's considerable wealth allowed Aline to travel through Europe after finishing school, where she pursued her interest in the theater. She wanted to be an actress and spent a year studying with Eleanora Duse who advised her to try her hand at production instead. She continued studying in Europe and there, produced her first play before coming back to the burgeoning little theater movement taking place in America. During the 1914-1915 season, the aspiring producer presented four plays at her theater in the Fine Arts Building in Chicago.

In August of 1914, Taliesin, Frank Lloyd Wright's beloved country home near Spring Green, Wisconsin, was burned to the ground by a deranged family servant. Seven people were killed, including Wright's companion, Mamah Cheney, and her two children. Anguished and devastated, the architect turned to work as his solace, focusing on rebuilding Taliesin and on other projects which included a Glencoe housing development and the Imperial Hotel in Tokyo. When Aline Barnsdall approached him at the end of that fateful year, he welcomed the opportunity to work with her and began a series of sketches for an avant-garde Barnsdall Theatre. However, Wright completed only preliminary drawings when his client set off for California to visit two major expositions in San Diego and San Francisco.

An avid traveler, Aline Barnsdall never stayed long in one locale before going to another. Her trip to the West Coast convinced her that California was the place to be, and she decided to build her theater in San Francisco instead of Chicago. Her plan was to form a traveling company to

"Miss Aline Barnsdall turned this beautiful site, Olive Hill, over to me as a basis on which we were to work together to build under the serene blue canopy of California."

AN AUTOBIOGRAPHY, Frank Lloyd Wright

30   present plays along the California coast and then build a permanent theater if she was successful. She wrote to Wright from Mill Valley, urging him to finish his work on the theater plans as soon as possible. She told him she was ready to buy land, and wanted to know what size lot to look for and approximately how much it would all cost. But her search for a theater site in San Francisco was frustrating, and during the summer of 1916, she went to Los Angeles and started a company called the Los Angeles Little Theater.

The season opened on October 31, 1916, with a production of "Nju" played before a glamorous audience of Hollywood luminaries that included Gloria Swanson, Theda Bara, Douglas Fairbanks, Charlie Chaplin and Harold Lloyd. The artistic director was Richard Ordynski, a handsome Polish expatriate who had trained with Max Reinhardt in Europe and was hired by Barnsdall for the entire season. The working relationship between them soon turned to a romantic one, but in spite of the fact that she became pregnant, Barnsdall made it clear to Ordynski that marriage was not an option. At the beginning of 1917, after the last play of the Los Angeles Little Theater season was performed, Ordynski left for New York where he was hired as stage director by the Metropolitan Opera Company. On February 27, 1917, Barnsdall's father died, leaving an estate appraised at over twelve million dollars to be divided equally between Aline and her younger sister Frances. In August of that year, Aline Elizabeth Barnsdall was born, and all of the heiress' energies became focused on her baby daughter and on the complicated paperwork of settling her father's will. The Los Angeles Little Theater season was over, and she decided to dissolve the company. She was thirty-five years old with a new baby and a huge fortune. It was time to make some changes in her life.

When Barnsdall bought Olive Hill in 1919, she and Wright had been working together on a set of preliminary drawings for a theater for almost three years. However, her priorities shifted when she acquired the 36-acre property, and she decided to first build a residence for herself and her small daughter. She wanted the house located on the summit of the hill, and Wright drew it with a verdant grove of tall trees as a background to the east and with vast views extending out over the Hollywood Hills and across the Pacific Ocean. His previously conceived sketches, drawn between 1916 and 1918 before he saw the property, were enigmatically appropriate for this particular Southern California setting. Barnsdall had pre-named her residence Hollyhock House and wanted Wright to incorporate abstractions of her favorite flower into his designs. Expansively, she envisioned a theatrical community on her splendid new property, and in addition to the main house and theater, she commissioned her architect to add a Director's House and an Actor's Abode.

Wright sketched his first master plan in pencil over a topographic map of Olive Hill. Working within the parameters set by the existing geometric grid of olive trees and curving access roads that formed the footprint of the land, Wright established an axial organization of the buildings. Hollyhock House was drawn as a quadrangle encompassing an inner court and gardens. The upper walls were pitched at 85 degrees to form parapets that would surround a roof garden. Monumental in scale, the house was experimental for Wright at the time, an anomaly that combined aspects of Italian villas, Mayan temples and his own Prairie houses in the Midwest. To achieve its singular style he specified many of the materials he would utilize in the decade ahead for the Ennis, Storer, Freeman and Millard California houses. The bearing walls of hollow terra-cotta tiles and upper walls of wood were clad in a cement stucco finish to be stained the soft gray-green of the olive trees. Art-stone, a darker and heavier mixture of cement, granite and gravel, would serve both structurally over surfaced concrete work such as columns, sills, bases, and fireplaces, and decoratively for the stylized abstractions of Hollyhocks that are a motif powerfully reiterated throughout the house. Wright thought of his use of Art-stone as "integral ornament" and used it extensively as a unifying theme.

The Olive Hill terrain also provided Wright with a

Columns are abstractions of the hollyhock, Aline Barnsdall's favorite flower.

"But as a creator you would spend my whole fortune
to create a perfect thing—it is the nature of creation."
Aline Barnsdall, in a letter to Frank Lloyd Wright

32

natural path for a manmade watercourse of meandering streams, ponds and waterfalls that cascaded down to the bottom of the hill. Similar to the elements he had explored at Taliesin in 1910 and would use successfully throughout his career, his lavish implementation of water organically linked together the earth and his bold new architecture. He termed the innovative style concept *California Romanza* and often spoke of it as a vacation from the machine-age dictates to which he had always adhered. His prolific output of drawings for Hollyhock House reflect an exhilarating freedom from convention as he continued his designs for the open vistas and sunny climate of the California landscape. However, by the end of the year, Aline Barnsdall had grown impatient with the lack of progress on Olive Hill and complained to Wright that her project was being neglected because of his long absences from the site as he traveled back and forth to Japan for his work on the Imperial Hotel. Wright's solution was to send his eldest son Lloyd, who had been working on the plans for Olive Hill from the studio at Taliesin, to supervise the project and to get construction underway.

Lloyd Wright was a logical choice to take over as superintendent for the Barnsdall project. Trained by his father in Oak Park and in Europe, he came to California in 1911 to work in San Diego and Los Angeles with Irving Gill. He returned to Taliesin and continued working on his father's projects, including Olive Hill. His lovely wash perspective drawings of Hollyhock House convey his familiarity with the building and illustrate it as sculpted into the crown of the hill, a long, low residence of palatial proportions. He arrived in Los Angeles in December of 1919, and immediately began a search for a reliable contractor, hoping to get the house into construction by May or June. He drew a planting plan, specifying appropriate trees for the grove behind the hill indicated on his father's drawings. When he found that the house's working drawings lacked sufficient detail to get construction bids, he hired a local draftsman to upgrade them and mailed others back to R.M. Schindler, then an assistant

at Taliesen and involved in the Olive Hill project, for clarification. He hired S.G.H. Robertson as general contractor and also worked with Barnsdall's business advisor, Clarence Thomas. Ground was broken on April 28, 1920, but within a few months tempers flared, and all of the principals were battling with each other and with sub-contractors, tradespeople and city officials.

In August of 1920, Frank Lloyd Wright came to Los Angeles to meet with his client, who, because of spiraling costs, had written that she felt he was sacrificing her fortune to his art. She was concerned with creating income and wanted to change the entire master plan, adding a commercial zone of stores, rental housing and perhaps a movie theater to her property along Hollywood Boulevard. Wright, Sr. went back to his studio and redesigned the scheme to include all of the changes and adjustments Barnsdall had requested.

But the trouble on the hill escalated, and according to Eric Wright, Lloyd Wright's son, an incident occurred that made it impossible for his father to continue as supervisor. A fierce argument over the cement work on one of the pools led one of the contractor's to come at his father with an axe, and Wright threw him into the unfinished pond. Soon after the fracas, Frank Lloyd Wright decided to bring Rudolf Schindler to California, and in December of 1920, they both arrived at Olive Hill. Wright, Sr. had brought along the finished Master Plan II and assigned the revised work to the two men before he sailed again for Japan. Schindler was to oversee the buildings and Lloyd Wright would continue with all of the landscaping including the existing olive orchard, grading the sites, and the construction of roads.

R.M. Schindler, the Viennese architect who was to become world famous in the years ahead, had seen and admired a portfolio of Wright's while working in Berlin, and contacted him when he came to America. He had worked as an assistant to Wright since 1918 and was involved with Olive Hill from its inception. But instead of helping the situation there, his antagonistic attitude caused new problems

Cement stucco walls were stained the soft gray green of the olive trees.

and aggravated old ones. Aline Barnsdall left for Europe, announcing that she would not come back until her residence was completely finished. Wright promised her that from July 14th to July 30th, he would personally supervise the finishing touches on Hollyhock House and that he would bring order to the chaos that seemed to reign on Olive Hill. There is no written record of when Barnsdall moved into her new home or how long she stayed. Within two years, she was traveling again and had decided to give Hollyhock House to the City of Los Angeles.

BARNSDALL PARK
in memory of
THEODORE N. BARNSDALL
1851–1917

Our fathers mined for the gold of this country
We should mine for its beauty. ALINE BARNSDALL

This plaque was installed by Barnsdall to honor her father soon after she deeded Hollyhock House to the City of Los Angeles. Although the gift of her home and surrounding acreage at the crown of Olive Hill was initially rejected in March 1924 by the Los Angeles City Council, it was formally accepted by the Board of Park Commissioners on January 3, 1927, and leased for fifteen years to the California Art Club. In July, she made a second gift of Residence "A" to the City and stipulated that it be used for children's classes in dancing and music. Barnsdall kept the only remaining building on

Olive Hill, the Director's House, or Residence "B", for her personal use when she was in Los Angeles. She hired Rudolf Schindler to remodel it to fit her needs, adding a suite with bedroom and bath over the garage. It was here that she died of a heart attack, alone with her pet dogs, on December 18, 1946. Residence "B" was demolished in 1954.

In 1995 the Barnsdall Park Master Plan was prepared for the City of Los Angeles Department of Recreation and Parks, addressing the general principles stated by the Planning and Development Committee of the Barnsdall Park Board of Overseers. The comprehensive plan focuses on capturing the original charm of Olive Hill, with Frank Lloyd Wright's concept of "the land as the beginning of architecture," as the unifying principle. Using early topography maps and landscape drawings, the environmental restoration will focus on landscaping the access roads, contouring the land, and planting additional olive trees. A new commercial development of shops and cafes will serve as a community link between Barnsdall Park and a new Metro Station. At the end of summer 1999, Hollyhock House was closed for repairs and remodeling, including retrofitting the building to bring it up to Los Angeles Earthquake Codes. Current plans project an opening date of spring 2001. During the construction period, the Los Angeles Municipal Art Gallery will offer a continuing exhibit of Hollyhock House with relevant information including videos of the ongoing renovation; architectural models; historic photographs; and an installation of furniture designed by Frank Lloyd Wright.

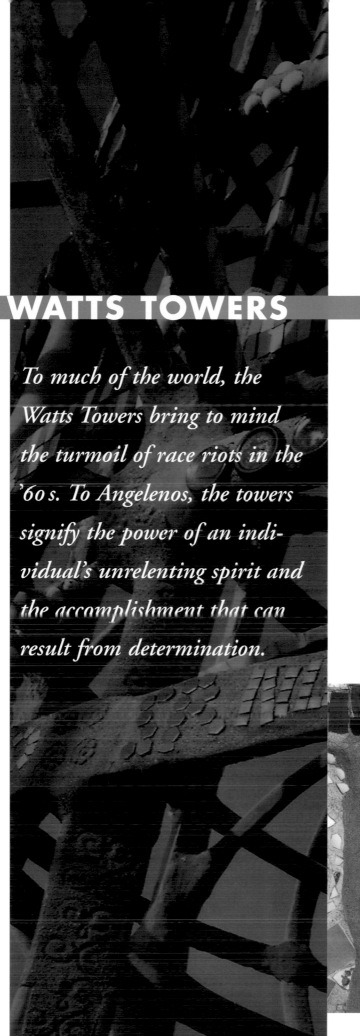

WATTS TOWERS

To much of the world, the Watts Towers bring to mind the turmoil of race riots in the '60s. To Angelenos, the towers signify the power of an individual's unrelenting spirit and the accomplishment that can result from determination.

There is a small triangular lot on a quiet dead end street in a primarily residential section of Watts that holds the mystical monument known throughout the world as the Watts Towers.

On its 1/10th of an acre surface, measuring 155 x 138 x 69 feet, seventeen structures stand. The three tallest towers are 99 feet, 6 inches; 97 feet, 10 inches and 55 feet, respectively. There are several smaller versions, 15 to 30 feet high, as well as a dazzling assortment of fountains, birdbaths, pavilions, patios, an outdoor oven, a garden made of cement cactus, an openwork gazebo with its own 40-foot spire, a small replica of a sailing ship built into the prow of the triangle and a scalloped enclosing wall. The entire assemblage is adorned with the palette of Rodia's found art: sparkles of blue and green glass, shards of patterned pottery, classic tiles

Inlaid found art on the scalloped enclosing wall

"Watts Towers Withstand Torture Test"

1959 Headline, UCLA LIBRARIAN

from the early days of Malibu, and seashells salvaged from the Pacific ocean shore, are all pressed with painterly precision into the cement skin that covers the steel and wire mesh skeletal structures beneath it. It took 34 years for Simon Rodia to single-handedly create this historic masterwork, and his awesome accomplishment has achieved international recognition as a controversial work of art.

It was a Saturday afternoon in October and the Watts Towers, threatened with demolition by the city of Los Angeles, were about to undergo a dramatic and carefully calculated stress analysis test. A crowd of people— reporters, television crews, Watts residents and citizens from all over the city—waited apprehensively for the trial of the Towers to begin. Devised by N.J. Bud Goldstone, an aeronautical engineer with North American Aviation, the pull test was to prove to the Department of Building and Safety that the Watts Towers were indeed safe and not an "unauthorized public hazard" as they had claimed.

The test was scrupulously planned by Goldstone and his colleagues, a team of technical experts including engineers and architects. With donated funds raised by the Committee for Simon Rodia's Towers in Watts, they had installed the necessary heavy equipment and electronic apparatus. Working with the tallest spire, a 70-foot scaffold went up the north side and many of the sculptural bands and columns of the 100-foot structure were wrapped in protective padding. On a 33-foot platform, a hydraulic cylinder was connected by steel cables to the tower and to a winch truck at a distance of 150 feet. Because the City's main concern for safety had crystallized around the towers' resistance to wind pressure, Goldstone's experiment had been designed to simulate a pull on the tower equal to the force of an 80 mile per hour wind.

When a critical load of 10,000 pounds was applied gradually in 1,000 pound increments, the tower held fast, easily withstanding the agreed upon tension. However, the steel beam connecting the tower to the hydraulic cylinder began to bend and the testing was called to a halt; the tower was stronger than the equipment brought in to test it. Simon

LEFT   *Threatened with demolition, the Towers undergo a stress analysis test.*
ABOVE *One of a bedazzling assortment of fountains, birdbaths, pavilions and patios on the property*

Rodia's singular structure had remained unscathed by the sophisticated stress test, dropping only a single seashell in response to the arduous efforts to pull it down.

The enthusiastically partisan crowd cheered as the slender spire was released, and it became clear that the City's 1957 order to "remove these dangerous towers" would no longer require compliance. A jubilant Committee accepted the red "unsafe" sign from the head of the Department of Building and Safety, aware that Rodia's masterpiece had survived not only the stress test, but also the bureaucratic battles it had endured as well. They had fought City Hall and won.

"The Rodia Towers in Watts and Watts itself have often shared the same fate in the city to which they belong. Both have suffered frequent neglect and stubborn indifference, relieved by spasmodic episodes of concern."

THE WATTS TOWERS OF LOS ANGELES, Leon Whiteson

38

Simon Rodia, a.k.a. Simon Rodilla, Sam Rodia, Don Simon and Sabatino Rodia, was born Sabato Rodia on February 12, 1879, in southern Italy, in the small village of Ribottoli and was probably named for the nearby Sabato River. The village was in the region of Campania and close to the town of Nola, where the three-day Festa de Giglio was held each summer. The festival dated back to the Middle Ages and featured a religious procession in which three-ton ceremonial towers, fifty to sixty feet high, were carried on the shoulders of Nola's citizenry to celebrate the town's patron saint. Historians consider it likely that the impressive image of these towers was subliminally imprinted on Rodia as a child, influencing his future work.

At the age of fourteen, Rodia sailed to America to join his older brother, Ricardo, in a Pennsylvania coal mining town. There, he took on a series of jobs as a day laborer in logging and mining camps and gained a reputation as a reliable worker. When Ricardo was killed in a mine explosion, Sabato left Pennsylvania for the West Coast. For the next twenty-five years, he drifted from Seattle to Oakland to Texas to Long Beach, marrying three times along the way. He had three children with his first wife, one of whom died at an early age, and he remained estranged from the surviving two all of his life. Over the years, moving gypsy-like across the country, Rodia held jobs as a construction worker, night watchman, telephone repairman, cement finisher and tile setter. Finally, around 1921, he purchased the small house and lot at 1765 East 105th Street in the City of Watts that became the site of the Towers and settled down with his third wife, Carmen, to begin to build his structures.

The shabby clapboard house on its open lot was subject to dirt and grime blowing in from all sides and from the rattling vibrations of the Big Red Cars and the Southern Pacific freight trains that regularly rumbled past on the railroad tracks just thirty feet away. Carmen soon fled the noisy and unpleasant setting where her husband was obsessively engaged in building his towers, working an eight hour day as a tile setter and coming home to work far into the night

as well as on weekends. When she left, she took his few meager possessions with her, including a phonograph and a stack of recordings of his cherished Italian operas. Rodia was forty-one years old, alone, and about to embark on the Herculean task of making something out of nothing.

He was a small man with big hands; his diminutive size determined the span of the towers' interstices, which could only be as high as his arms could reach. He climbed about his structures like a spider on a steel web, using no scaffolding, carrying whatever he needed for the task at hand in a bucket over his arm and in a burlap bag at his waist. Strapping himself into a makeshift window-washer's belt, or fitting his body into a piece of bent steel hooked to the tower rungs, he worked on the rib above him. When he had finished the section to his satisfaction, he would move on to another project, leaving the first one to thoroughly dry and harden so that he could use it as a ladder rung to work on the next horizontal bar. He first assembled his work on the ground, using no written plans or specifications. All of this was accomplished without the aid of bolts, rivets or welds, using simple tools such as a hammer, pincers and pliers.

His foundations were surprisingly shallow, only 18 inches deep for the tallest tower. They were filled with cement mortar into which steel rods were inserted deep into the ground to become the main vertical support columns. These rods were wound tightly with wire mesh and chicken wire and then packed and covered with mortar, all of which hardened into an effective form of reinforced concrete. Buckminster Fuller, a bemused admirer of the untrained Rodia's uncanny abilities as a structural engineer, commented on his use of mesh-wrapped steel enclosed in thin concrete as a brilliant adaptation of what was known to professionals as ferro-cement construction. The bases of the tallest towers were weighted down with heavy pieces of broken concrete, and anchored into the surrounding 4-inch thick patio floor. Rodia's insightful construction methods allowed the towers to sway with the wind and to withstand the same 1933 Long Beach earthquake that cracked the

TOP, LEFT   *According to Buckminster Fuller, the structures are a marvel of intuitive engineering.*

TOP, RIGHT   *The Towers were built with simple tools, without the aid of bolts, rivets or welds.*

ABOVE   *Rodia named his installation "Nuestro Pueblo," "Our Town," and imprinted it on the entry gate.*

Simon Rodia. Photograph by Sanford Roth, c. 1955

foundations of Los Angeles City Hall. Sometime after the earthquake, Rodia decided to further stabilize his structures with additional weight at their bases and with outside columns and numerous intersecting rings to act as braces between the towers. As sturdy and resilient as the man who made them, the structures are a marvel of intuitive engineering. He named his installation "Nuestro Pueblo," "Our Town," and imprinted it on the main gate and several times on the tallest tower.

Glittering and gleaming on every exposed surface of these amazing steel constructions are bits and pieces of the collected paraphernalia of Rodia's life. He chose from an eclectic aggregation of found objects that included glass, mirrors, marble, rocks, assorted seashells including abalone, mussel and clam, ceramic tile, pottery, tableware, linoleum and discarded pots and pans. In a 1953 documentary photographed by USC film-student William Hale, the diminu-

tive Rodia walks along the railroad tracks near his home picking up the rocks, stones and shards of glass that later adorn his work. He would often take the Big Red Cars to the beach, bringing along a couple of empty cement bags to gather whatever he saw as possible art from the shoreline.

The glass is predominantly green and blue, with some amber from wine and beer bottles. The green glass is derived almost exclusively from 7-UP bottles and the blue from Phillip's Milk of Magnesia bottles and Noxema cream jars. Many of the architectural tiles are from Malibu Potteries where he worked and probably took home broken and rejected pieces, and from other companies including Batchelder Tile. The tableware, broken and whole, includes Fiesta and Harlequin, Bauer, Metlox, Catalina and Canton Ware. In addition, small surprises such as miniature dolls, horses, unicorns and a golden bumble bee are used in the work. Most of the materials were in everyday use circa 1920

"Simon Rodia's clustered towers in Watts are unlike anything else
in the world - especially unlike all the various prototypes that
have been proposed for them by historians who have never seen
them in physical fact. Their actual presence is testimony
to a genuinely original creative spirit."

LOS ANGELES: THE ARCHITECTURE OF FOUR ECOLOGIES, Reyner Banham

to 1950 and are historically interesting artifacts in themselves. Rodia would lay the objects out on his workbench where he could study them before making a choice. Applying these found treasures to the towers involved a creative process that some have compared to the pointillism of George Seurat or to the assemblage art of Ed Keinholz. Two decades earlier in Barcelona, Antonio Gaudi had created remarkably similar ornate mosaics on his buildings which Rodia could not have copied because he had never seen them. When he was shown illustrations of Gaudi's work at a 1961 Berkeley conference in his honor, he asked if the architect had had helpers. When told that Gaudi had many, Rodia smiled and said, "I never had no help at all."

Incredibly, this hugely creative process went on for 34 years until in 1955, Rodia put down his tools for the last time and decided it was time to go. He gave away the deed to his land and everything on it to a neighbor, Leon Saucedo, and went to live near relatives in Martinez, California. There is much conjecture but little known fact as to why Rodia chose this time to abandon his work and his life on East 107th Street. Reading between the lines of his heavily accented and sometimes deliberately obfuscating conversation, it seems clear that he left with reluctance, sadness and a heavy heart.

In Calvin Trillin's 1965 *New Yorker* article, a Watts neighbor is quoted as saying, "But the new kids in the neighborhood started bothering him. They'd throw rocks at him and call him crazy." Rodia himself told a visitor, "Los Angeles is in danger. Kids run round, break things, throw rocks. They watch me at night. When I go to the picture show, they come. When I come home, window broken, door broken." His new home in the small town of Martinez was two small rooms in a boarding house where he spent his days roaming the town or sitting in the sun near the rail yards. When Watts Towers committee members went to talk with him, he was reluctant to discuss his sudden departure. But one statement, ruefully made in answer to an interviewer's invitation to return to the Towers, shed light on the mystery. "Dear young lady, I am too old," he said politely, "I broke my heart there."

In August of 1965, the tragic conflagration known as the Watts riots occurred in the same disenfranchised neighborhood of South Central Los Angeles that is home to Simon Rodia's Watts Towers. In spite of widespread damage throughout the area, the Towers remained untouched. However, they had been subjected to periodic vandalism and mindless assault after Rodia left in 1954, and a year later, the house on the triangular lot burned to the ground. In 1959, two young champions of the neglected Towers, William Cartright and Nicholas King, bought the property for $3,000. They formed the Committee for Simon Rodia's Towers in Watts (CSRTW) to protect and preserve the property and to act as diligent fundraisers for its maintenance.

After the Committee's successful 1959 load test saved the Towers from demolition, they began a long and arduous struggle to repair and to maintain the vulnerable structures in the best possible condition. They ran out of money in 1975 and decided to deed the property to the City of Los Angeles. In May of 1978, the City of Los Angeles deeded the Towers to the State of California on a 50-year leaseback provision. Bill AB 990 was approved by the California State Assembly in 1980, appropriating a million dollars for the Towers restoration. After the 1994 Northridge earthquake, an additional million dollars was granted by the United States Federal Emergency Management Agency. Over the years, the Watts Towers and its dedicated protectors have been embroiled in numerous conflicts with rotating bureaucracies including a lengthy litigation that was finally settled in 1985. Designated as Los Angeles Cultural Heritage Monument #15 and as a National Landmark, the complex has grown to include the Watts Towers Art Center of the Los Angeles Cultural Affairs Department which hosts children's workshops, art exhibits, lectures and an annual jazz festival. Currently an expert restoration team is engaged in an extensive renovation of the Towers which will reopen to the public in the year 2002.

41

HOLLYWOOD BOWL

Now in its 70s, the Hollywood Bowl is an integral part of Los Angeles culture. Originally designed by Lloyd Wright and renovated by Frank Gehry, its shell-like shape, spherical hanging speakers and natural setting epitomize Southern California's outdoor lifestyle.

It was known as Bolton Canyon, the chaparral, sage and Indian paintbrush covered natural amphitheatre that would become the site of the Hollywood Bowl. Located at the junction of Cahuenga Boulevard and Highland Avenue near the Cahuenga Pass, the Bowl is situated in the midst of California history. On his trek across the land to establish a string of missions, Father Junipero Serra paused there to intone a Sunday Mass; and in 1769, Gaspar de Portola crossed the Pass on his expedition from Mexico City to Monterey. In a formal ceremony in the vicinity of the Bowl, Governor Andreas Pico and Col. John C. Fremont signed a treaty in 1847, ending the Mexican regime in California. In May of 1848, Kit Carson brought the first overland mail from the east to California through the Cahuenga Pass.

Discovered in 1919 by a father and son team after three weeks of traipsing over the rambling Hollywood hills, the small enclosed valley of Bolton Canyon seemed perfect for an outdoor theater. "My enthusiasm knew no bounds," Ellis Reed said. "Immediately I wanted to test the acoustics. I scaled a barbed-wire fence, went up to the brow of a hill. Dad stood near a live oak in the center of the bowl-shaped area and we had a conversation with each other." Although they spoke in low tones, every word could be heard clearly, and the two men knew they had found an ideal sylvan setting that would resonate with sound.

H. Ellis Reed, a traveling Shakespearean player, and his father, Walter Reed, had been assigned the task of finding a place for a cultural center in the Hollywood Hills by the Theater Arts Alliance. Walter Reed later became Bowl superintendent, a post he held until his death. The Theater Arts Alliance was incorporated on May 26, 1919, to form a community park and art center. The Alliance was an outgrowth of the American Pageantry movement of the early 1900s, and carried forward its idealistic principles of bringing art and beauty to the people and making it accessible in a community center. In keeping with this philosophy, the Alliance wanted its center to be in the democratic setting of an outdoor environment. In a 1918 book titled "The Open Air Theater," art critic Sheldon Cheney posited that the classic Greek theater represented the ideal juxtaposition of nature and man, the primal forces of each melding together to form an alchemy of art.

The parcel of land Ellis and Walter Reed found consisted of 58.57 acres and was owned by three separate parties who agreed to option their acreage to the Theatre Alliance for a total of $50,000. Wealthy heiress Myra Hershey owned 50 acres she called Daisy Dell, which she sold for $20,000. Mrs. Edith Teale owned a home at the entrance to the site which she sold to the Alliance for $7,500. The last parcel was situated on what is now the seating area of the Bowl. The owner, James Lacy, operated a dry cleaning business on the property which the Alliance purchased for $20,000.

After a heated period of infighting between members as to the eventual use of the property, the Alliance disbanded and reorganized under the name "The Community Park and Art Association" on October 25th, 1920. The newly organized group finally acquired the property for $65,000, the extra 15,000 covering the expenses incurred in the ongoing negotiations. However, in 1924, The Community Park and Art Association reincorporated into the Hollywood Bowl Association and deeded the land to the County of Los Angeles because of increasingly high property taxes. The County accepted the proposal subject to a 99-year lease at one dollar per year.

Created in the years between two World Wars, the current Bowl was carved out of the conflicting views of its long list of illustrious sponsors and benefactors, each of whom had a vision of what the Bowl should be and an agenda for implementation. The delicate balance between the art form, the setting and the audience was a daunting challenge, and shaping an environmental architecture that would address this trinity of needs has always been an ultimate goal.

The first commissioned architect, Louis Christian Mullgardt, prepared development plans for the Hollywood Bowl in the summer of 1919. His initial drawings were rejected by Theater Arts Alliance board president Christine Stevenson, and although he continued to work with the board for several years, his scheme was eventually abandoned due to his million dollar construction costs. In addition, some of the board members objected to the elaborate nature of his design which they felt was inappropriate for the Bowl's rustic background. It was not until the first season of board member Artie Mason Carter's "Symphonies Under The Stars" that minor improvements such as enhancing the landscaping and grading the hillsides were implemented.

On a mild California summer evening in the early 1920s, five thousand people came by automobile, on the Big Red Streetcars or on foot, walking up the dusty lane lined with light-strung pepper trees that led into the Hollywood Bowl. The natural environment was intact, except for some

*"My message to you is that the tremendous undertaking
of giving the summer concerts during a period of ten
weeks beginning July 11, was not born of self-greed or
commercialism, but is an outgrowth of community faith."*
Artie Mason Carter, President, Hollywood Bowl Association

Outline of new Bowl appears as construction begins in Bolton Canyon.

Overhead view of the Bowl in relation to the Hollywood Freeway, 1954

"There is probably no other place on earth where, within an urban area, 18,000 people can gather in a natural amphitheater, oblivious to the pressures of the city just outside their park-like sanctuary."
Ernest Fleischmann

sparse plantings and an attempt at sloping the hill. The audience sat on temporary wooden benches or settled down on blankets spread out on the ground of the flat seating area in front of the makeshift stage. There was as yet no Shell, and the orchestra was assembled on a crude proscenium made of a wooden platform with a pine wood back. This was enclosed with canvas along the sides and across the top.

It was July 11, 1922, and the first concert of the "Symphonics Under The Stars" was about to begin. The Governor of California, William D. Stephens, welcomed the audience and officially opened the season. Mayor George Cryer introduced conductor Dr. Alfred Hertz, the popular and ebullient conductor who would lead the Los Angeles Philharmonic Orchestra in a rousing rendition of Wagner's Overture to Reinzi. Thirty concerts were offered that year, with tickets selling at the reduced price of twenty five cents a seat to encourage community participation. The bargain seats were so succesful that the 1922 season had a record attendance of 150,000 people, and Artie Mason Carter's concept of "Symphonies Under The Stars" was succesfully launched.

In 1923, Aline Barnsdall, oil heiress and patron of the arts, became an active member of the Hollywood Bowl Association board. Her substantial donations during her four year tenure helped the organization to fund the 1923 season; to retire the outstanding debt on the mortgage in 1924; and to begin construction and landscaping improvements in 1925. Barnsdall played a significant role in the Bowl's future because of her enthusiasm for art and architecture and her long affiliation with Frank Lloyd Wright. Since 1919 Wright had been designing Barnsdall's home and arts complex on a 36-acre site in Hollywood known then as Olive Hill. Working with him at Olive Hill was his son, Lloyd Wright, Jr., whose designs would lead to what has become the Bowl's famous and often emulated shell.

With Barnsdall's contributions augmented by a fund of $300,000 from the County of Los Angeles, Allied Architects, a cooperative association of local Los Angeles architects, was commissioned to draw up plans for major renovations at the Bowl in 1926. Myron Hunt, architect for the Pasadena Rose Bowl, worked with the firm of Robertson and Bergstrom on the project, and it was he who created the parabolic shape of the Bowl that opens like a fan into the surrounding hills. Permanent seating was installed on a substructure of concrete and steel. At the base of this dramatic ellipse was the orchestra pit and the concrete stage under which Hunt built substructures for dressing rooms and storage. Rimmed along the periphery with massive stairways, the new amphitheater was well-anchored in its site and embraced its natural surroundings.

On June 22, 1926, this "new" Bowl was dedicated with a gala program that featured soloists and conductors, as well as an impressive gathering of 24 pianists all playing together on the open stage. Another pre-opening event was the presentation of C. W. Cadman's spectacular American Indian opera, "Shawnewis," with an authentic Indian princess named Tsianini singing the soprano lead.

It was during this season that Hunt designed the Bowl's first Shell, a curvilinear structure decorated with Oriental landscape paintings, that enclosed the orchestra in an arched proscenium. Although it worked well for the musicians, the concave Shell, combined with the new seating and stage improvements, distributed the sound inefficiently and changed the perfect natural acoustics of the Bowl site. This Shell was deemed unsatisfactory by the Board because of its sound distortion, and in 1927, Aline Barnsdall brought in Lloyd Wright, Jr. to replace it.

Perhaps most famous today for his spectacular Wayfarer's Chapel in Laguna Beach, Wright was the eldest son of Frank Lloyd Wright and was trained by his father in Oak Park, Illinois. He came to California in 1911 to work with Irving Gill and others, eventually branching out into the world of film set design. In 1917, he became head of Paramount Studios Art Department, working over the years with such fabled film designers as Cedric Gibbons and Norman Bel Geddes.

His affiliation with the Hollywood Bowl began in 1926 when he worked on the Allied Architects project preparing studies for general landscaping and designing an entrance drive. These plans were not accepted by the board, but recognizing his experience and skill as an architect and designer, Wright was asked to create the sets for the 1926 season's closing production, Gordon Craig's presentation of "Julius Caesar." His splendid open-air designs were so appropriate for the setting that the board invited him back for the first production of the 1927 season, an operetta version of "Robin Hood" written by Reginald De Koven. It was at this point that the board gave Wright the commission to create a new shell.

Working with Bowl superintendent H. Ellis Reed, the man who had originally discovered the amphitheater's natural acoustics, Wright utilized discarded lumber and plaster board from his dismantled "Robin Hood" production to build a pyramid shaped edifice. This shell, created in ten days at the nominal cost of $1,500, was an acoustical masterpiece, a carefully engineered structure of direct lines which Wright had worked out mathematically to achieve a quality of sound that rivaled the original acoustics lost through construction and grading. The flat sections of the pyramid reflected and evenly distributed sound from all of the musicians in the orchestra. The echos created by the previous shell were eliminated by sound traps formed by diagonal braces in the slanted lateral walls. Critics of the time compared the shell to an Indian teepee or a Mayan Temple, but Wright thought of it as a simulacrum of the American Southwest.

This temporary shell was considered too radical for the taste of many of the Bowl's concertgoers, and the Board decided to replace it with a second, hopefully more permanent structure. Because of Wright's past acoustical accomplishments, they chose him to design a new shell once again for the 1928 season, with the admonition that it be more conventional this time. Working within the restrictions imposed by the semicircular form mandated by the Board, Wright created an elegant edifice that became a symbol of

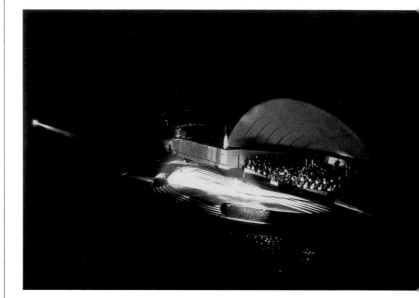

TOP   *Lloyd Wright's elliptical shell*
ABOVE   *Traditional Easter sunrise services at the Hollywood Bowl*

Moderne architecture. The elliptical shell, made of nine pre-fabricated arched segments that formed the gracefully curved structure, could be disassembled and stored at the end of each season. To create a tension similar to that of a piano sounding board, he used overlapping ten-foot ring sections, made of wood for resonance, tied together with steel rods and turnbuckles. Acoustically superb, Wright's second shell projected sound to the entire audience.

Due to a series of misunderstandings, the 1928 shell was not stored over the winter and as a result it weathered and showed signs of deterioration. In December, the Board hired an engineer to assess the damage and on his recommendation, the shell was demolished. Allied Architects was called in to design the shell for the 1929 season, and it is this landmark structure, a reworking of Wright's last shell, that is still in use today. It was constructed of light airplane steel covered with transite, a material made of cement and asbestos and considered to be fireproof and waterproof. Mounted on ball bearing wheels over a set of tracks, it was designed to be movable so that the stage could be cleared when necessary. However, the new structure weighed 55 tons and eventually crushed the wheels into the tracks. Although the wheels were replaced, the problems persisted and the shell hasn't been mobile since the 1960s. The new shell was clearly an attractive adaptation of the one that went before it, but the hardened transite created an echo that interfered with sound projection, and it soon became clear that it was not up to Wright's acoustical standards.

In 1970, Ernest Fleischmann, general director of the Hollywood Bowl, asked Los Angeles architect Frank O. Gehry to explore innovative methods to enhance the acoustics. Gehry, with acoustician Christopher Jaffee, devised an ingenious temporary modification to the existing 1929 shell, installing within it an arrangement of sonotubes that would help to broadcast the sound out to the audience. These cardboard sonotubes, ordinarily used in architecture as forms for concrete columns, were replaced yearly. In 1980, working this time with acoustics expert Abe Melzer, Gehry conceived of the extraordinary fiberglass spheres that are suspended from the ceiling inside the shell. The positions of the hollow spheres were arranged in varying heights and sizes calculated to improve the acoustical properties for the orchestra. In 1981, Gehry added 150 loudspeakers throughout the amphitheater, wrapping the entire canyon in a quality of sound that can be appreciated by every concertgoer in the audience.

Since 1992 and the passage of Proposition A, the Bowl has received over 43 million dollars to be used for restoration of the 120-acre site, and Phase 1 of the planned construction was completed in 1995. The architecture of the shell has remained basically intact, although it is probable that modifications will continue to be made to accommodate future changes in the acoustics. The roster of celebrities who have appeared within its famous shell include internationally renowned conductors and performers ranging from Igor Stravinsky to Luciano Pavoratti, as well as such legendary pop stars as The Beatles, Judy Garland, Frank Sinatra, and Barbra Streisand. Now in its 70s, the Hollywood Bowl continues to be an integral part of Los Angeles culture, a quintessential amphitheater set in a Southern California canyon that has become a prototype throughout the world.

LOS ANGELES CITY HALL

Originally the tallest building in Los Angeles, City Hall was the unifying focal point of a rapidly expanding metropolis. Today, the building punctuates the downtown cityscape with its graceful form and isolation from the highrise activity of the central business district.

In 1918, Mayor Frederick T. Woodman appointed a committee headed by William Mulholland, Chief Engineer for the city's Public Service Department, to look into downtown sites suitable for a comprehensive civic center for Los Angeles. The city was being shaped by industrial interests and developers with little or no thought to the eventual configuration of the growing metropolis, and the planning commission knew that Los Angeles required a central location for its administrative and cultural facilities. The original Los Angeles Plaza under Spanish rule had been designed in accordance with their Laws of the Indies as a community meeting place, a locale for social gathering. At the beginning of the twentieth century, Los Angeles city planners wanted a civic

Rendering of an early version of City Hall

Council Chamber

Sketch of Mayor's Office
New City Hall

LEFT, TOP   *Perspective of Council Chambers, c. 1926*
LEFT   *Perspective of Mayor's Office, c. 1926*
ABOVE   *Steel skeleton of the tower under construction, May 3, 1927*
OPPOSITE   *Overview of the entire construction site, September 14, 1926*

"Its broad and solid base is typical of the City's firm foundation at the strategic point of the great Southwest; the flanking wings rising from the base typify to its marvelous growth from the original pueblo; while the soaring lines of the tower symbolize the indomitable spirit of its citizens that made it possible."

Los Angeles City Hall, 1928, George P. Hales

TOP   *Los Angeles City Hall dedication day took place on April 25, 1928.*

ABOVE   *Los Angeles "The Magic City," Booklet, 1930*

core that would become the nucleus of the far flung city, situating museums, libraries and city office buildings together in a pivotal location that would bring cohesion to what was fast becoming a random and scattered municipality.

This vision of a unifying focal point for civic buildings was based on the ideas of a national movement known as City Beautiful, and in 1903, an art committee was established in Los Angeles to negotiate with builders, developers and planners for the location and aesthetics of proposed civic improvements. This committee, which became the Municipal Arts Commission and later the Cultural Affairs Commission, hired Charles Mulford Robinson to design a civic plan for the city. Robinson, a Rochester, New York city planner and representative of the City Beautiful movement, published his strategy for Los Angeles in 1909, situating the civic center at Spring and Temple Streets with an administrative center, a public library, and a museum approached through a colonnaded Court of Honor. Robinson's plan was never implemented, but many of his original ideas were incorporated into the various plans that followed.

Mayor Woodman's 1918 committee incorporated many of the City Beautiful principles espoused by Robinson's plan into their evaluations of alternate sites for the new civic center. After an extended search and heated public debate, they advocated the area known as the old Temple Market Block as the best possible site for an administrative center, and recommended the removal of the existing Romanesque County Courthouse to make way for separate administrative and cultural complexes. Approved by the city planners, the matter was also formally accepted by Angelenos in a 1923 bond issue designating 7.5 million dollars to build the civic center, including a new City Hall, on a large downtown parcel of land bounded by First Street, Hill Street, Los Angeles Street and Sunset Boulevard.

During the 1920s, several competing proposals for the administrative center were considered by the City Planning Commission. Soon after the electorate passed the bond issue in 1923, a comprehensive design in Classical style was sub-

mitted by landscape architects W. D. Cook and George D. Hall. Hall, a graduate of L'Ecole des Beaux Arts in Paris, envisioned a monumental and formal civic center based on a north-south axis. The firm's preliminary drawings presented a towering and symmetrical Hall of Administration at the back of which was a forecourt leading to a union railroad terminal. On one side of the tower-like building was a city hall and on the other, several government buildings with Greco-Roman colonnades along the front. The Cook and Hall plan preserved the historic Los Angeles Plaza, enclosing it in a circular park. Spring Street, Main Street and Broadway were widened to one hundred foot thoroughfares that connected with First Street and Sunset Boulevard, providing adequate surfaces for automobile traffic.

One of the most impressive schemes presented to the City Planning Commission was the 1924 Administration Center plan submitted by the Allied Architects Association of Los Angeles. Designed on an east-west axis, the square mile site positioned lots along First Street, Temple Street and Sunset Boulevard. Bunker Hill was developed as a scenic park to the west, and the Plaza was protected as an historic Los Angeles landmark to the east. Streets that ran north and south on the drawings were depressed below grade to isolate traffic and separate cars from buildings and pedestrians. The Hall of Justice on this Allied Architects plan, a fourteen-story building clad in gray granite, is the only completed Beaux Arts building from any of the early civic center plans submitted to the City Planning Commission that survives today as an exemplar of architecture of the early twentieth century.

The two leading rivals for the Los Angeles Civic Center commission soon became the subject of contentious debate between city officials, the planning commission, and each other. Allied Architects claimed that the north-south axis of the Cook and Hall plan lacked architectural integrity, that it offered too little open space, and was generally uninspired; Cook and Hall said that the Allied Architects plan was impractical, required too much land, was far too expensive, and the east-west axis cut off the northern mountain views.

The Southern California Chapter of the American Institute of Architects chose Allied Architects' design and convinced the Board of Supervisors to accept its plan. At this point, the Los Angeles City Council intervened, and ordered that the new City Hall be built in accordance with the design plans of Cook and Hall. The ensuing deadlock was referred to the City and the Regional Planning Commissions with an admonition to reach a compromise between the two plans that satisfied all involved parties. The resulting agreement, based on an urban policy that primarily protected development, business and political interests, satisfied no one, but it was officially adopted by city and county officials in 1927. The continuing controversy over the truncated plan's many shortcomings prevailed, and it was never implemented. The only buildings constructed during the 1920s were the Hall of Justice and City Hall, and when the Hollywood Freeway was built, it ran right through the original Cook and Hall civic landscape. In the following decades, other public buildings were built within the projected district, but the idealistic goal of unified centrality was never achieved. In the midst of this lengthy and polemical struggle, plans were being made to build a new Los Angeles City Hall on city-owned land on Spring Street to replace the 1888 Romanesque Revival City Hall located at the southwestern edge of downtown.

The Native Sons of the Golden West had the honor on June 22, 1927, of laying the cornerstone for Los Angeles City Hall at a festive ceremony that took place near the building's main entrance at 200 North Spring Street. Its contents included copies of local newspapers for that date, a 1927-28 City budget, and a Los Angeles telephone directory. To set the cornerstone, a symbolic mortar was mixed containing quintessential California elements; samples of sand from every county beach, cement mined from all over the state and water taken from each of the twenty-one Missions.

In 1925, three of the city's leading architects, John C. Austin, John Parkinson and Albert C. Martin Sr., were commissioned to begin an extensive set of preliminary drawings. Once the plans were completed and approved by city and county officials, the building was begun on a fast track schedule with the general contractors starting operations, breaking ground, pouring foundations, and commencing the steel framework by July of the same year. The site boundaries were Spring Street on the west, Main Street on the east, First Street on the south and Temple Street on the north, an area approximately 338 feet east and west, and 770 feet north and south. The architects wanted to create a building that was free from the constraints of any particular style of architecture, and John C. Austin wrote in 1928 that their design, with its stepped back tower and flanking wings, was "Modern American," a prescient concept that anticipated the Moderne movement. It is probable that the overall design was influenced by Bertram G. Goodhue's earlier Nebraska State Capitol, a building with a skyscraper tower set on a classically designed base. Los Angeles City Hall was a departure from the plethora of Beaux Arts buildings in downtown Los Angeles, an eclectic concoction with Art Deco sensibilities that soared above the city as its tallest building until the height limit was rescinded in 1957.

An historic photo of the building under construction taken in the summer of 1927, shows a mammoth steel skeleton thrusting upward into the sky from a sturdy base, flanked by wings extending out at the third floor level. The stepped-back tower dominated the steel silhouette of City Hall, rising to a pyramidal roof 452 feet above street level. At its apex, the Colonel Charles A. Lindbergh Airway Beacon was later installed with two lamps and an automatic switching device to insure that its light would constantly illuminate the city. Designed as an independent structure, the tower is anchored in reinforced concrete to its own foundation and is braced in both directions. The architects installed compressible joints in the outer walls of each story to allow for expansion, contraction and oscillation, a sensible precaution in an earthquake-prone region. The City Hall skeleton contained over 8000 tons of structural steel with a floor area of 856,000 square feet and the underground garage had a capacity of 550 automobiles.

LEFT, TOP *City Hall colonnade*
LEFT *Entrance lobby with its inlaid mosaic floor*
ABOVE *City Hall colonnade*

Aerial view of City Hall and the surrounding civic buildings, c. 1941

Completed a year later, the building's exterior facades were clad in gleaming white California granite, and the metal grills facing the large arched windows of the first story were finished in a contrasting gray-green. Spanish tiles were used to roof the two flanking wings on either side of the tower. At the building's main entrance on Spring Street, two broad flights of granite steps led up to a colonnaded forecourt with Romanesque arches, and arcaded passages on both sides of the forecourt provide access to the secondary entrances. All of the construction materials used in the courtyard area—tile, granite, brick and cement—were produced in California, and the solid cast bronze entry doors and lighting fixtures were manufactured in Los Angeles. The building's ornate interior was designed by Austin Whittlesey, and its four-story Byzantine Rotunda, 70,000 square feet of marble-clad halls, lobbies and public rooms attest to his ability to interpret the needs of a prestigious public building.

Los Angeles City Hall Dedication Day took place on April 25, 1928. Thirty-two thousand Angelenos attended festivities that included a luncheon at the Biltmore Hotel; a reception for visiting dignitaries; an "Historical Pageantry" tableau put on by Hollywood showman Sid Grauman; an official dedication ceremony led by film producer Joseph Schenck and the sudden and dazzling illumination of the monolithic building with searchlights donated by MGM Studios. As a finale, President Calvin Coolidge pressed a telegraph key from his office at the White House to turn on the light in the Charles A. Lindbergh Airway Beacon at the apex of the City Hall Tower. At the President's touch, one of Los Angeles' great landmark buildings was officially inaugurated.

In 1986, Project Restore was founded to preserve the architectural heritage of Los Angeles' historic civic landmarks. Plans were underway for a seismic upgrade of City Hall when the 6.7 Northridge earthquake jolted Los Angeles in 1994, causing substantial damage to the building. The majority of the tenants were relocated so that renovations could begin, and in 1998, the building was completely vacated for an extensive rehabilitation project, closing down Los Angeles City Hall for the first time in its 73-year history. The latest innovations in seismic retrofitting were used to bring the structure up to code, including the installation of 500 base isolators under the building so that it could move horizontally during a quake, and new shear walls were positioned within the existing walls of the central tower to strengthen the building's structural integrity. In addition to the earthquake retrofit, four major public areas are undergoing restoration at the present time; the City Council Chambers, the Board of Public Works Session Room, the 27th Floor Observation Room, and public access areas such as the elevators, corridors and lobbies. The building's exterior terra cotta tiles are being cleaned and repaired, and the contours of the new landscaping on the South Lawn is planned for informal gatherings and public functions. The Project's seismic and historic design teams (led by A.C. Martin Partners) are working to prepare City Hall for a gala opening sometime in the year 2001.

GRAUMAN'S CHINESE THEATRE

"Grauman's Chinese Theatre is an example of an era in Hollywood that will never be surpassed. It is the zenith of exotic architecture, familiar to millions the world over."

LOS ANGELES HISTORIC-CULTURAL MONUMENT #55, JUNE 5, 1968, CITY OF LOS ANGELES CULTURAL HERITAGE BOARD

NOTHING CAN FALL ON YOU BUT CANVAS IF THERE IS ANOTHER QUAKE!, proclaimed a sign hand-printed by Sid Grauman for his family's Tent Theatre soon after the 1906 San Francisco earthquake. Officially known as Grauman's National, the hastily assembled theatre consisted of one projector, a huge tent leased from a traveling evangelist, wooden pews salvaged from the rubble of a demolished church, and several rolls of undamaged film purchased from an Oakland dealer. All of this was set up on Market Street on the grounds of the burned out Unique Theatre, the small vaudeville house with 800 kitchen chairs for seating and a single piano for music, that the Graumans had been successfully running from the early 1900s. Featuring such performers as Al Jolson, Sophie Tucker and Fatty Arbuckle, the Unique was one of several family-owned theaters the Graumans had

Vintage view of Grauman's Chinese Theatre from Hollywood Boulevard

ABOVE *Exterior façade of forty-foot walls is crowned by a bronze pagoda roof.*
OPPOSITE *Searchlights fill the night sky at the gala premiere of* Hell's Angels.

acquired since moving to San Francisco from Alaska, where they had gone to look for gold and failed to find it. Their early success in San Francisco was the beginning of a lengthy era of fame and fortune in the movie business, and Sid's ingenuity and innate ability as a showman was a precursor of things to come. Because the new Grauman's Tent Theatre was one of the first business enterprises to get back on its feet after the earthquake, providing a valuable service to the devastated population of the chaotic city, San Francisco honored the Graumans with an award for civic contribution.

David and Rosa Grauman's son was born on St. Patrick's Day, March 17, 1879, and they chose his middle name in honor of the holiday. Sidney Patrick Grauman grew up in Indianapolis, Indiana, where his father was a minstrel man in vaudeville earning a meager living by traveling with the show circuit and performing in small venues across the country. In 1898 when the gold rush was just hitting the news, they took off for the Klondike and settled in the town of Dawson. There, David Grauman continued to perform while his young son sold newspapers to help earn enough money to get by. Within two years, the family had done well enough to move to San Francisco and operate a small chain of theaters, beginning with the ill-fated Unique. It was at this small vaudeville house that Sid Grauman was first captivated by movies when he saw *The Great Train Robbery*. The feature-length motion picture of oncoming trains and gunfighter's bullets that seemed to come toward the camera delighted the audiences who ducked from the shocking illusions on the screen. Soon after, Grauman convinced his father to add movies to the Unique's regular programming. Although all of the family's theatres burned to the ground in the raging fires that followed the 1906 earthquake, they quickly recouped their losses, first with the Tent Theatre, and then with several other movie and vaudeville houses, including the Empress, an 1800 seat all-concrete building on Market Street in downtown San Francisco.

However, it became clear to the Graumans that Los Angeles was the developing movie capital of the world,

Huge octagonal columns establish the immensity of the theater's interior space, c. 1927.

"It's ironic that in Hollywood where history is written on the wind and where our product deteriorates with time...the cement in Grauman's forecourt is the only lasting memorial to artists who've made Hollywood famous."

Hedda Hopper, LOS ANGELES TIMES columnist, 1953

the place in which exhibition houses could grow and flourish. In 1917, Jesse L. Lasky, a film producer and friend of the family, arranged a meeting between Sid and the head of Paramount Pictures, Adolph Zukor. The deal was that Zukor would buy out the Grauman interests in San Francisco and finance the construction of a new theater in Los Angeles which Sid would manage as part owner. Originally called the Rialto, the impressive 2,345 seat theater the Graumans built with Zukor at the corner of Third and Broadway in downtown Los Angeles became Grauman's Million Dollar Theatre, playing to capacity crowds. Elaborately Spanish Colonial in style, the building's trademark was the huge ornate terra cotta arch over the Broadway entrance. This successful venture was followed by Grauman's Metropolitan Theatre at Sixth and Hill, across the street from the Biltmore Hotel. Decorated with exotic Middle Eastern ornamentation, the huge Metropolitan could seat 3,485 moviegoers, and was the largest theater ever built in Los Angeles. While the Metropolitan was still under construction, Sid Grauman was working with the architectural firm of Meyer & Holler on his next theater, the Egyptian, this time in the boom town of Hollywood. When it opened in 1922 with the premiere of Douglas Fairbanks Jr's *Robin Hood*, King Tutankhamen's tomb had just been making headlines, an opportunity for a publicity tie-in that Sid Grauman, the inveterate showman, fully exploited to promote the dramatic Egyptian Revival architectural style of his newest venture. The theater on Hollywood Boulevard was sited at the end of a long courtyard lined with tombstones, ending at an armed guard in full Egyptian regalia walking back and forth on the roof parapet. All of this activity by the renowned entrepreneur took place within five years, during which time he managed and maintained the Grauman movie theaters with his distinctive flair and style.

It began with a ground-breaking ceremony featuring movie stars Norma Talmadge and Anna May Wong digging dirt with a golden shovel for the foundation of Grauman's Chinese Theatre on Hollywood Boulevard at Orchid

Avenue. Sid Grauman had sold out his interest in the downtown theaters to the group headed by Adolph Zukor, the Paramount/Famous Players-Lasky organization, retaining only the Egyptian in Hollywood as he launched his plans to build his most ambitious undertaking. His partners were Joseph M. Schenck and C.E. Toberman, with Meyer & Holler, the same architectural and engineering team that had so successfully built the Egyptian, designing, interpreting and constructing Sid Grauman's dream of ultimate Oriental grandeur. They began with an analysis of the floor plans of more than 200 existing theaters, incorporating the best features of each into a compatible whole. Thousands of photographs of Chinese art and architecture were studied for ideas and authenticity, and Raymond Kennedy, an architect with Meyer & Holler, produced a series of black and white drawings interpreting the interior and exterior design possibilities. The 2,258-seat theater was completed within a year, the smallest details of the entire project scrutinized by the eagle eye of its perfectionist creator who fashioned a flamboyant Chinese fantasy world that has endured as one of the greatest motion picture palaces.

The famous elliptical forecourt leading into the theater, where some say Sid himself accidentally clumped through a patch of wet cement and got the idea for celebrity footprints, is flanked by an exterior facade of forty-foot walls crowned by a towering bronze pagoda roof painted jade green. Planted with fully grown palms and tropical trees, the imposing entry simulated an exotic garden in a Chinese temple, an impression enhanced by a pair of massive stone-carved "Heaven Dogs" at each side of the main entrance. These Ming Dynasty stone sculptures were believed by the ancients to ward off evil spirits and were imported from China by Sid Grauman, along with many other authentic art treasures he installed throughout the lavishly decorated theater.

Inside the building, the color scheme included varying shades of Chinese red, ranging from ruby and scarlet to crimson and coral. Contributing to the interior's overwhelming sense of splendor were the auditorium's brick walls lacquered red with an overlay of silvery birds and trees; the pale yellow silk velvet stage curtain scrolled with a matching design of silver foliage; the red leatherette seats with black and gold cushions that echoed the baroque ceiling's red, gold, black and ivory tones; the carpets with a Chinese dragon theme woven in Hong Kong; the Chinese lanterns in the orchestra pit that changed colors during the overture; and overall, the profusion of Oriental art pieces and furnishings strategically placed in every available space of the theater lobby and auditorium. The final magical Grauman touch was the scent of sandalwood that somehow wafted everywhere inside and outside the theater.

All of the seats were positioned on a raked floor plan with a gradual elevation from the stage to the lobby level at the back of the house, providing patrons with optimum viewing—a plan Grauman had successfully used in previous theaters. The central mezzanine at the back provided space for the projection booth and Sid Grauman's private box which he named the Cathay Lounge. Along each side of the auditorium, a row of huge octagonal marble columns, seven feet in diameter and extending to the height of the ceiling, established the immensity of the vast interior space. The stage hydraulics featured a floor built in sections that could drop to a twenty-foot pit beneath and was one of the largest in the world at 165 feet wide, 71 feet high and 48 feet deep. The architects installed an auxiliary dynamo system that made the theater complex independent of outside electricity, providing it with sufficient power to function entirely on its own. Grauman characteristically and tirelessly promoted the theater and its innovations all during the construction period. By the time of its spectacular opening in 1927. Grauman's Chinese was already a legend in its own time. The premiere of Cecil B. DeMille's *The King Of Kings*, preceded by one of Grauman's famous live Prologues in tableau form, attracted thousands of spectators who filled the new forecourt and spilled out onto Hollywood Boulevard and the surrounding streets. Dazzled by the arcing searchlights and the passing parade of movie stars and celebrities that included (according to the opening night program) governors, mayors, generals, judges and millionaires, the crowd became an integral part of a typical Grauman extravaganza; the essential Everyman background for all the royals attending the evening's opulent festivities.

The first four cement slabs were already in place for the opening night celebration, bearing the footprints, handprints, autographs and salutations of screen star Norma Talmadge; swashbuckling Douglas Fairbanks; Mary Pickford, America's sweetheart at the time; and Sid Grauman, the man who first conceived the notion. These original artifacts from 1927, though faint and rubbed away by time, are still located along the curb of Hollywood Boulevard in front of the theater. One of the greatest publicity stunts ever created by a man who was famous for them, the ritual honor of putting prints down for posterity in wet cement soon became a coveted glittering prize of the movie stars and remains so to the present time. The footprint ceremonies at premieres helped to open many of Hollywood's greatest hits and quickly caught on with the general public. It was a time before television, when a night or a matinee at the movies for the price of a 25-cent ticket was the preferred form of entertainment, and the reigning stars were royalty sought out by moviegoers with autograph books in hand. Crowds began showing up at Grauman's forecourt to see the growing number of cement slabs representing their favorites, and today, over 2,000,000 tourists a year make the pilgrimage to the famous Hollywood mecca to touch and to try their own feet in the celebrated footprints of the stars. Although most of the great luminaries of the past decades can still be found there, a dark rumor persists that buried somewhere in the basement under Grauman's Chinese Theatre are a number of rejected squares that have been quietly dug up and replaced with more enduring recipients, a sad but typical form of Hollywood archaeology.

*"Showmanship is like any other merchandising. You must buy
desirable material, present it to advantage and price it right.
And above all, you must let the world know what you have."*
Sid Grauman

Early Hollywood days at Grauman's

In April of 1929, Sid Grauman sold his interest in his
landmark theater to the Fox West Coast organization at a
healthy profit, announcing that he would remain in an advisory capacity. But when the stock market crash hit in
October of that year, he lost almost all of his $6,000,000
fortune, mainly because his broker could not reach him in
his suite at the Ambassador Hotel. Grauman, who was an
insomniac, had standing orders with the switchboard not to
disturb him before noon, and by that time, it was too late to
recoup his losses. He continued to be affiliated with the
Chinese Theatre in various capacities throughout his lifetime, although he was no longer an owner of his illustrious
creation. In 1973, Ted Mann bought the National General
Corporation's chain of theaters, including Grauman's
Chinese, for $67,500,000. He changed the name to Mann's
Chinese Theater and built two smaller movie houses on
adjacent property, the Chinese II and the Chinese III, and
in 1984, installed George Lucas' THX Sound System in all
three theaters.

Sid Grauman received several honors before his death
in 1950, including a Special Oscar statuette presented to him
at the 21st Academy Awards, the only time in the Academy's
history that an exhibitor was honored by the Academy of
Motion Picture Arts and Sciences, and a testimonial dinner
sponsored by the Hollywood Chamber of Commerce at
which his friend, Joseph Schenck, introduced Sid as the
greatest showman of them all. A few weeks after he died on
March 5, 1950, the California State Assembly passed a resolu-
tion stating, "Be it resolved by the Assembly of the State
of California that members of the Assembly express extreme
regret for the passing of Sid Grauman, one of the truly
great showmen of this state." Grauman's Chinese Theatre is
his living legacy, a powerful monument of fantasy architecture that exemplifies a halcyon time in the annals of
Hollywood history.

67

GRIFFITH OBSERVATORY

"Anchored at the junction between earth and sky, Griffith Observatory presides over the entire Los Angeles basin. Its Thirties Moderne styling allies it with Hollywood, but at Griffith Observatory, the stars are the stars."

E.C. Krupp, Director
Griffith Observatory

The image is indelibly dramatic: Natalie Wood and James Dean caught forever in adolescent angst against the cosmic background of the Griffith Observatory. *Rebel Without A Cause* is one of many movies shot at the Observatory over the years and to this day, it remains a favored location for cinematographers. Set into the highest promontory of the southern slope of Mt. Hollywood, the Art Deco building with its crown of three copper domes was the gift of Colonel Griffith W. Griffith. The Colonel, who had donated the 4,000-acre Griffith Park to the city of Los Angeles in 1896, was deeply interested in astronomy and was an active member of the Southern California Academy of Sciences. His first sight of the night sky through the telescope on Mt. Wilson expanded his awareness of the universe and motivated him to share his enlightenment with the public. His gift of

Forty-foot concrete obelisk commemorates six of the world's great scientists.

GRIFFITH OBSERVATORY
Los Angeles, Calif.
The Wm. Simpson Construction Co., Contractors.
John C. Austin & Frederic M. Ashley, Architects.
THIS PHOTO MADE 10-1-33

TOP   *Construction began on October 7, 1933, and was completed in nineteen months.*

ABOVE   *Griffith Observatory's three steel-framed domes are clad in shining copper.*

OPPOSITE   *Interior view of the octagonal foyer*

*"The architects of the Griffith Planetarium have at
last made me a favorable offer for my collaboration."*
Russell W. Porter

$100,000, pledged on December 12, 1912, was designated for
the construction of a community observatory, a non-profit
educational institution to be completed and functional by
1915. Rather than a research facility, he envisioned a publicly
accessible place with telescopes and other scientifically-
oriented amenities.

Some community leaders were suspicious of Colonel
Griffith's ongoing generosity, believing it to be a quest for
social redemption because of a personal scandal. Griffith shot
his wife Tina in the eye during a drunken rage, wounding
but not killing her. His famous criminal attorney, Earl
Rogers, argued a new defense of "alcoholic insanity," winning a lenient verdict of "assault with a deadly weapon" for
Griffith who was sentenced to two years in San Quentin and
a $5,000 fine." The City Council was skeptical of Griffith's
plans and wanted to use the money to achieve its own priorities, an athletic field and clubhouse on the park grounds. In
1914, Mayor Henry R. Rose intervened and appointed Col.
Griffith as head of a three-man committee to construct the
observatory as well as the Greek Theater. Site preparation
had begun on the Greek Theater when construction came to
an abrupt halt as three park commissioners sued Griffith, his
committee, the Mayor and the City of Los Angeles over
power lines in the park.

At this time another observatory scheme was brought
before the Board of Park Commissioners by Colonel Louis
Ginger. Originally conceived in 1902 by Colonel James W.
Eddy, the designer of Angel's Flight on Bunker Hill, the plan
consisted of a 2,000-foot funicular railway leading up to several public facilities, including an observatory, at the top of
Mt. Hollywood. It was rejected at the time due to excessive
construction costs, but with the substantial pledge of
$500,000, the new syndicate led by Ginger proposed bring-
ing Eddy's dream to reality. The city council and park
commissioners preferred this project to Griffith's, and construction on his observatory was further delayed as a result.
Realizing that the observatory was not likely to be built in

his lifetime, Griffith changed his will in 1916, stating,
"I direct that the remainder of the trust funds shall be used
and expended towards the erection and completion of a Hall
of Science and Observatory, to be constructed upon Mount
Hollywood in said Griffith Park." The Colonel died in
1919, and it was not until April of 1930 that the Griffith Trust
announced plans to begin the process of construction of his
observatory.

Over the years, Griffith had become involved with the
Throop Polytechnic Institute, renamed the California
Institute of Technology (Caltech), and consulted with its
president, James A.B. Scherer, as well as other prominent

astronomers including George Ellery Hale who was to develop the 200-inch telescope on Mt. Palomar. When the Griffith Trust formed the Technical Advisory Committee to get the project off the ground, it enlisted the brainpower of some of these men along with Caltech president, Dr. Robert Millikan; Dr. Edward Kurth, a Caltech scientist; Dr. Mars Baumgardt, a Griffith advisor; and Dr. Walter S. Adams of Mt. Wilson Observatory. The first order of business was the choice of an architect.

Competitors for the enterprise included modernist Richard J. Neutra; John Parkinson and Donald B. Parkinson, the father and son team who would design Union Station a few years later; and the firm of Austin and Ashley, who were unanimously selected by a 4-0 vote of the Park Commission. Known for their design of the recently completed Los Angeles City Hall, John C. Austin and Frederic M. Ashley had already established themselves in the architectural community. However, the firm had no experience in observatory design and made the wise decision to hire someone who did as a consultant.

Between 1930 and 1933, Russell Porter's prolific drawings of the observatory and its various facilities ranged from expansively flamboyant to thoughtfully practical, an amazing range of original ideas that demonstrated his deep understanding of the factors involved. Porter was an amateur astronomer who wrote a column for *Scientific American* on telescope construction. His expertise was such that famed astronomer George Hale contacted him in 1928 to collaborate on the 200-inch telescope for Mt. Palomar. Later, when the Technical Advisory Committee of the Griffith Trust sought out an expert to do a series of conceptual drawings of their emerging ideas, it was the visionary Porter that committee member Hale recommended.

Realizing the extent of Porter's contribution to the future project, the newly commissioned architectural firm of Austin and Ashley bought up all of his existing drawings and hired him as a design consultant. It is arguable that Porter's original concepts, including the striking three-domed exte-rior, formed the basis of the final architectural plans adopted by the Technical Advisory Committee. These plans incorporated the specific stipulations set forth in Colonel Griffith's will, focusing on a Hall of Science, a Planetarium Theater, a rooftop promenade, and the space for public telescopes. It was to be clad in concrete, "to endure for the ages," as Griffith stated. However, his wish that the observatory be built at the top of Mt. Hollywood presented an unanticipated financial and engineering problem.

The site was 60 feet long by 20 feet wide, too small to accommodate the structure without significant grading. In addition, there was the problem of parking which would require a larger pad at the top or three graded terraces just below, according to an April 1931 engineering assessment. Two alternate sites on Mt. Hollywood were considered: a slope facing eastward toward Glendale, and the south-facing slope overlooking the Los Angeles basin. Architects Austin and Ashley chose the latter, stating it had "the most advantages at the least expenditure."

Once the new site had been chosen, Van Griffith, Colonel Griffith's son, led a coalition consisting of the Griffith Trust, the Park Department and the Park Commissioner in an effort to break the Colonel's will. A "friendly" suit was filed, and Van Griffith explained to Superior Court Judge Albert Lee Stephens that the original site on the highest peak that his father had specified in 1912 had become impractical and expensive in 1931, and on November 14th, the judge gave his approval for the change of location to the lower elevation.

Construction of the Griffith Observatory finally began on October 7, 1933, fourteen years after the Colonel's death, and was completed nineteen months later at a cost of approximately $655,000. The building's form was strongly influenced by its unique function, and the new observatory incorporated almost all of the ideas for the "evolutionary museum" that Griffith had envisioned from the beginning. Although it officially opened on May 14, 1935, with a gala evening ceremony, it was at ten a.m. the next morning that

Set into the south-facing slope of Mt. Hollywood, the Observatory overlooks the Los Angeles basin.

TOP   *The building's form was strongly influenced by its unique function.*
ABOVE   *James Dean and Natalie Wood in front of the Observatory in* Rebel Without a Cause

*"It is my suggestion that said Hall of Science should provide
for a large moving picture theater or hall, having a seating
capacity for many people."*

Colonel Griffith J. Griffith, Last Will and Testament, February 8, 1916

the gray concrete building with its radiant copper domes opened to the general public. As guest director, Dr. Philip Fox introduced the wonders of science the new observatory offered to the people of Los Angeles. It was clear that Griffith's idealistic fantasy had at last become a reality.

That first morning, visitors strolled across the front lawn to view the Astronomer's Monument, a 40-foot tall concrete obelisk commemorating six of the world's great scientists. They entered the observatory through the Main Rotunda to see the Foucault Pendulum swinging from above, demonstrating Earth's rotation on its axis. Surrounding the octagonal foyer and painted across its ceiling were elegant Hugo Ballin murals, heroic depictions of the advancement of science over the ages. In the West Rotunda they looked through the "triple-beam coelostat," three solar telescopes on one mounting that offered three different views of the sun. They climbed staircases on either side of the building to the rooftop promenade for a panoramic view of the city of Los Angeles, or to see the impressive 12-inch Zeiss refractor telescope imported from Jena, Germany. But from the beginning, the most impressive exhibition by far was the Planetarium Theater.

One of the first optical planetarium installations in the world at the time of the opening in 1935, the round 510-seat theater became an instant favorite for visitors to the new facility. In total darkness, the Zeiss projector presented time-traveling star shows overhead on the hemispheric dome of the 75-foot diameter ceiling. Visitors gazed up at various representations of the night sky, encountering virtual reality before it was invented, as they witnessed the motion of the sun, moon, and planets in ancient times and far into the future. The drama of the universe was acted out across the simulated darkness above them, a profound experience that continues to attract multitudes of people to Griffith Observatory. Close to 50,000 school children a year visit the Planetarium to see the live multimedia shows presented by a skilled lecturer.

Over the years, Griffith Observatory attendance has grown steadily to the point of two million visitors per year. Although the copper domes were stripped and refurbished in 1985, no major renovations have been undertaken, partly because of the Observatory's designation as a Cultural Landmark and the resultant limitations on change. However, when Los Angeles voters passed Proposition A and Proposition K designating a total of 28 million dollars for the renovation and expansion of the Griffith Observatory, there were sufficient funds available to make the necessary improvements while staying within the exacting guidelines of historic preservation.

In 1990, a committee consisting of the Los Angeles Recreation and Parks Department, the observatory staff, the Friends of the Observatory (FOTO) and the Griffith Trust drew up a Master Plan to renovate, restore and preserve the observatory and raised additional funds. The three-phase plan includes renewal of the existing buildings and systems; the complete upgrading of the Planetarium including a new state-of-the-art computerized projector; and an expansion of 27,000 square feet of space including enlarged exhibit areas, staff offices, workshops, restrooms, bookshop and food service, all with improved handicapped access wherever possible. Additional parking facilities and an expanded observation deck at the northwest edge of the observatory are currently under consideration. Scheduled to open in August 2003, the 58 million dollar refurbishment (under the direction of architects Hardy Holzmann Pfeiffer and Brenda Levin) will carry forth Colonel Griffith's utopian dream that "all mankind looking through a telescope could revolutionize the world."

UNION STATION

Union Station's blend of mission and art deco architecture transports the modern day visitor to Los Angeles' past. When originally built, it was the epitome of modern time, welcoming passengers to an exploding metropolis full of dreams and promise.

Twenty minutes before noon on Wednesday, May 3rd, 1939, the parade celebrating the opening day festivities for Los Angeles Union Terminal began its trek down Alameda Street. Half a million people swarmed around the old Plaza area and filled the seats of the review stand that had been built between Aliso and Macy Streets. It had been a long and arduous battle to get the fabulous new Station, and Angelenos wanted to see it firsthand.

Dignitaries on horseback included Sheriff Biscailuz, Governor Culbert Olsen, Mayor Fletcher Bowron and film star Leo Carillo, all riding and waving to the music of ten marching bands. The parade's theme was the history of transportation, and examples of early California days such as covered wagons, stagecoaches and a pony express were

Fred Harvey restaurant at Union Station

78

TOP   *Union Station and the thirteen miles of rail line within the terminal*
ABOVE   *Opening day ceremonies featured antique locomotives draped in festive flags.*
RIGHT   *The Spanish Revival style reflects Los Angeles' ethnic heritage.*

"In presenting the new Union Station, we give you America's newest rail terminal. It marks another milestone of progress for all Southern California. Architecturally beautiful and typically Californian in aspect, the new depot is both spacious and ultra-modern in every facility of equipment and design."

Union Station Opening Day Brochure, 1939

followed by horse cars, pioneer trolleys and automobiles. Finally came three locomotives; Santa Fe's #5006, Union Pacific's #3939, and Southern Pacific's streamlined General Service, all draped in festive American flags.

At the rear of the station, a 6,000-seat amphitheatre was the setting for "Romance Of The Rails," a lavish production presented to sell out audiences several times a day as part of the opening ceremonies. Elaborately staged and costumed, the pageant depicted the history of the nation's railroads and traced their arduous path across the country. The three locomotives seen in the opening day parade rolled majestically along the tracks fronting the amphitheater for a rousing grand finale. The celebration continued until the following Sunday, when the Los Angeles Union Station officially opened for business.

It took twenty eight years and a monumental struggle to bring the Los Angeles Union Station through the law courts, off the drawing boards and into reality. The reasons for this difficulty were classic city politics versus private enterprise. Although everyone wanted a train terminal, no one wanted to pay for it, and it was only after exhaustive legal battles that the many parties involved arrived at a workable solution.

It began in 1911, when a city planner named Bion Arnold recommended to the Los Angeles City Council that a terminal be constructed by the three transcontinental railroads serving the city, the Sante Fe, the Southern Pacific, and the Los Angeles and Salt Lake (later combined as Union Pacific). Because there were no government subsidies available, it would be paid for by these railroads, a common practice at the time. The passenger depot would be a Union Station and represent the union of more than one railroad into a common facility. Just as other Union Stations had been built across the country as status symbols of the cities they served, Los Angeles' Union Passenger Terminal would be a gateway to the city, adding to its growing stature as a metropolitan center. The project would be an extension of the planned improvements for the Civic Center a few blocks away.

What started out as a bright civic dream developed into a gothic legal nightmare, dividing the city of Los Angeles into fiercely opposing factions at war with the cost-conscious railroads and each other. For fifteen years, the resulting legal complications were aired in such arenas as the California Railroad Commission, the Interstate Commerce Commission, The California Supreme Court, and finally the United States Supreme Court. The Los Angeles City Council turned it over to the people in 1926, placing two propositions on the April 30th municipal election ballot:

PROPOSITION 8: *Shall a union railway passenger terminal for all steam railroads be erected in the City of Los Angeles?*

PROPOSITION 9: *Shall a union railway passenger terminal for all steam railroads be constructed in the district bounded by Commercial Street, North Main Street, Redondo Street, Alhambra Avenue, and the Los Angeles River?*

This new development unleashed an accelerated war of words between its opponents—the recalcitrant railroads, and its proponents—the city government. Harry Chandler and the *Los Angeles Times* encouraged public support although most other publications seemed to side with the railroads. When the votes were counted the people of Los Angeles had approved both propositions; they wanted a Union Station and they wanted it adjacent to the city's historic beginnings as the Pueblo de Los Angeles at the Plaza site.

In spite of this Angeleno vote of confidence in the project, the City Council was compelled to continue its struggle with the railroad companies until all legal recourse was exhausted and the United States Supreme Court backed the Railroad Commission's mandate for a Union Station on May 18, 1931. On September 7, 1933, Mayor Frank L. Shaw, with the approval of the City Council, offered the railroads a million dollars (civic funds raised with a gas tax) toward construction costs if they would give up their opposition to the designated Plaza site. Stating that although he realized it was a more expensive parcel that the one preferred by the railroads, he felt that "the people of Los Angeles will not be

ABOVE   *Cavernous arched entries open into a vast five-story high interior.*

OPPOSITE *The waiting room's massive wrought iron chandeliers are ten feet in diameter and weigh 3,000 pounds.*

satisfied with the construction of the station on any location other than the Plaza site."

The railroad companies accepted this offer, ending the decades-long deadlock, and on October 4, 1933, the State Railroad Commission approved the "Plaza Set-Back" plan. Survey work was begun as well as construction on the 17-foot high fill which was required for the tracks. On December 4, 1935, twenty-four years after the idea was presented to the Los Angeles City Council, the final design was approved and bids were advertised for construction. Four years later at a cost of $11,000,000, Los Angeles Union Passenger Terminal was completed.

A collaborative team of architects worked together skillfully to create a Spanish Revival building of massive splendor that reflects Los Angeles' Spanish-Mexican heritage as well as the prevailing style of the 1930s, Streamline Moderne. Architects Donald B. Parkinson and John Parkinson, a father and son team well known in the city for such buildings as Bullocks Wilshire and Saks Fifth Avenue, consulted with a committee of architects from the three participating railroad companies including H.L. Gilman, J.H. Christie and R.J. Wirth.

The main station building extends 850 feet along Alameda Street and is distinguished by a singular 125-foot clock tower that sets it apart from other Mission style stations across the country. A cavernous double-arched entry dominates the building's clean exterior lines, opening into a vast 78,000 square foot interior space that is five stories high. Great wrought iron chandeliers, each ten feet in diameter and 3,000 pounds in weight, hang from the ceiling of the waiting room at regular intervals. The Spanish quarry tile that paves the walkways and corridors is inset with mosaic patterns of marble and travertine. The principal interior space is a cruciform, the length of the waiting room leading to the crossing width of the train platforms, with great halls like outstretched arms on either side. The north hall is the old ticket concourse, and the south hall leads to the original Fred Harvey restaurant with interiors by

architect Mary Elizabeth Jane Colter. On each side of the building is a spacious patio, lushly planted with indigenous trees and flowers by the original landscape architect Tommy Tomson.

There are ten train gates off the east end of the main waiting room. At its peak, Union Station used thirty-nine tracks in all, adding up to almost thirteen miles of rail line within the terminal. Eight tracks run along each side of the passenger platforms; five for railroad cars, six for switching facilities, eight for mail, baggage and express cars, three for engine release, and one that is used as a storage track. Overlooking this maze of railroad tracks are Terminal Tower and Mission Tower, both with electric locking devices to safely monitor the traffic flow.

The new Los Angeles Metro Rail subway system originates at Union Station, and access areas for the escalators to the subway boarding platforms are located just left of the main train tunnel and at the building's east entry. Traxx, an upscale restaurant and cocktail lounge, opened in December 1997. Catellus Development Corporation now owns Union Station and the land within its parameters. The company has plans for a major expansion in the coming years and has hired a preservationist to oversee current and future building projects in order to maintain the architectural integrity of one of the city's most cherished treasures.

TOP   *The Spanish quarry tile that paves the walkways and corridors is inset with marble and travertine mosaics.*

ABOVE   *Corridor between the terminal building entry and the Fred Harvey Restaurant*

THE LAX THEME BUILDING

Poised for flight within its steel cage of sculpted arches, the stationary spaceship that crowns the LAX Theme Building seems to wait for a chance to join the jets and take off into the wild blue yonder.

In 1928, the National Air Races were held at Mines Field, a sleepy Los Angeles airport situated on a pastoral sweep of agrarian fields where jack rabbits watched from the weeds alongside the runway. A truck farm occupied the west end of the runway and at the east end, a train railway spur had to be cleared by pilots for takeoffs and landings. This wide open rural setting of Southern California landscape officially became Los Angeles Airport on July 9, 1941, with the airfield used by the military during World War II. By 1947, five major commercial airlines—American, Western, TWA, United and Pan American—had begun their move from Burbank to Los Angeles. Today Los Angeles International Airport (LAX) is the third busiest terminal in the nation with more than 62 million passengers a year passing through the nine terminals that form the horseshoe of the now 3,600

The original rural Southern California setting of Mines Field was the site of the 1928 National Air Races.

86

TOP   *The original control tower, circa 1962*
ABOVE   *LAX circa 1962*
RIGHT   *Mines Field evolves into Los Angeles International Airport.*

"I encountered many discouragements and rebuffs, most of which were predicated upon my color. I survived a few financial hardships which might have been avoided had my face been white. But I do not regret these difficulties, for I think that I am a far better craftsman today than I would be if my course had been free."

AMERICAN MAGAZINE, Paul R. Williams

87

acre property. Three-fourths of Southern California's passenger and air cargo traffic go through LAX's 137 gates to traverse the 8 miles of runways that stretch across the massive airport.

At the epicenter of the airport's frenetic activity is the landmark LAX Theme Building, an enigmatic symbol of the Space Age dreams of the 1960s that captures the optimistic, techno-future envisioned at that time — a place that could easily have been a favorite hangout for George and Judy Jetson. Designed by Paul R. Williams in association with Pereira & Luckman and Welton Becket and Associates, the structure was initially conceived as the control tower of William Pereira's original futuristic scheme for a modern airport with elevated tramways, underground tunnels and parking, and glass domed bubbles with extended runways serving as terminals. But over a period of ten years, his "first airport of the Jet Age" was modified and adapted to the necessities of the rapidly expanding project, and a new control tower had already been built when Williams began construction on the Theme Building. By then it was 1960, and funding for the Theme Building came out of the $50 million overall Los Angeles Jet Age Terminal Construction Project which began that year.

Paul Williams had been working with the airport's architectural team for four years when he began construction on the Theme Building project in 1960. He had traveled a long and difficult road as a black man in an era of rampant discrimination to reach the commission of what he considered his signature building. Early in his career, the architect learned to sketch upside down so that his clients could avoid proximity and sit across from him. The first African-American member and eventually the first African-American Fellow of the American Institute of Architects, Williams was a smart, gentle and tactful man who managed to build a substantial practice in spite of the racism that permeated his time and marred his daily business dealings. Although he had designed prestigious buildings such as the Beverly Hills

Hotel and Saks Fifth Avenue as well as hundreds of palatial homes in Hancock Park, Holmby Hills, Beverly Hills and Pasadena, he never felt welcome as an equal in any of them.

Born in Los Angeles on February 18, 1894, Williams was orphaned at the age of four when his father and mother died within the same year. He and his brother were sent to separate foster families, and Paul was raised by the Clarkson family with a benevolent foster mother who taught him to always take the positive view in trying to attain his goals. Williams went to Polytechnic High School, the Los Angeles School of Art and the Los Angeles branch of the Beaux Arts Institute of Design. He entered the engineering school at USC and was a student there until 1919, although he never received a degree. To put himself through school, he designed and sold metal watch fobs and monograms for women's purses. He had a knack of winning every competition he entered, gaining confidence from each success.

While still in school, he worked in several architecture offices including: Wilbur D. Cook, where he learned landscape and town planning; Reginald D. Johnson, who specialized in residential design; and then the more commercial offices of John C. Austin, who became a mentor to the talented young designer. Here, Williams gained experience working on large projects such as the Los Angeles Chamber of Commerce, the First Congregational Church, the Shrine Civic Auditorium and the Hollywood Masonic Temple. Williams, who had simultaneously been studying for the state architectural exams, received his license in 1921 and opened his own office in the Stock Exchange Building in 1922. His former boss, John C. Austin, gave him a ninety thousand dollar residential commission to begin his independent practice. Williams had also obtained several other commissions for substantial homes in Flintridge and West Los Angeles. During a long and successful career, he designed what the client wanted, giving them large, comfortable, luxurious homes—architectural gems in English Tudor, Spanish Revival, or contemporary Colonial styles. His clients included millionaires and movie stars from E.L. Cord and Jay Paley, to Lucille Ball and Desi Arnaz, Cary Grant and Frank Sinatra. But it is the amazing achievement of his LAX Theme Building for which he will always be remembered.

Construction of the Theme Building began in April of 1960 and was completed in August of 1961 at a cost of $2.2 million. Approximately 900 tons of structural steel were required for the innovative building, and because the design of the supporting steel arches was a first, an unusual amount of steel falsework was constructed prior to the final erection of steel. Three temporary towers, each as tall as an eight-story building, were built to support the soaring parabolic arches while under construction. Kaiser Steel's Montebello Fabricating Division erected a steel skeleton that included four, 10-ton upper arch sections, each 105 feet long; four, 39-ton lower arch sections, each 107 feet long; four, 38-ton horizontal legs, each 83 feet long; and a 33-ton tension and compression ring six feet in diameter. Because of the enormous size of the steel sections, they were shipped to the site by truck during light traffic hours.

All of the steel work was fabricated around a reinforced concrete central core 85 feet high and 30 feet in diameter. The giant elliptical arches of steel weighed a total of 348 tons, and because of their density were erected in two sections; the lower sections welded to the horizontal legs which were attached to the central core and the upper arch sections welded to the lower sections and also at the top. The six-foot high tension and compression ring placed on the central column 70 feet above the ground helps to support the Theme Building's restaurant and observation deck, both of which are serviced by three passenger elevators and a freight elevator contained in the column. At 135 feet above ground level, the steel arches cross over each other creating fantastic interstices that frame the circular, flying saucer-like restaurant and the surrounding observation deck that provides a 360 degree view of the airport and the sprawl of Los Angeles beyond. Administrative offices, a kitchen and an employee cafeteria are built into the central core as well.

Poised for flight within its steel cage of sculpted arches, the stationary spaceship that crowns the Theme Building seems to wait for a chance to join the jets and take off into the wild blue yonder. Meanwhile, it is a gourmet restaurant named Encounter, with the intergalactic sensibilities of an early Star Trek episode. A 1997 renovation of the interior space was designed by Walt Disney Imagineering and features lava lamps, amoeba shapes, silver leather couches and three-dimensional walls with superimposed images of the moon's surface. The multicolored digitally woven carpeting and sculpted ceilings are highlighted with other-worldly blue and lavender light, as is the building's exterior. Although the restaurant does not revolve as many people mistakenly think it does, it offers spectacular views from almost any vantage point. Lush gardens designed by landscape architect Robert Herrick Carter surround the base of the building, and on display in the courtyard and lobby are lighted murals and commemorative plaques. Construction drawings depict the structure as a simple system of overlaid concentric circles. However, the LAX Theme Building was a revolutionary concept and continues to make a statement about what it represents: Los Angeles as an international city and gateway to the world.

"There is the matter of style versus design. Design concerns itself with the overall formal solution to a problem of building. But buildings too must wear a style that gives them an association to a certain period of time."

THE INFLUENCE OF PLANNING ON MAN'S DESTINY, Paul R. Williams

Paul Williams, FAIA and his Theme Building which captured the optomistic techno-future envisioned in the '60s.

CASE STUDY HOUSE #22

"Cantilevered acrobatically over the hillside into thin air above a shimmering Los Angeles, Case Study House #22 was the house heard 'round the world. Architect Pierre Koenig suspended disbelief along with gravity when he designed the daring, transparent structure, capturing in a single building what modern life in a modern house could be."

STUDY IN STEEL,
Joseph Giovannini,
Elle Decor

When Buck Stahl met Pierre Koenig he had no clue that he was about to commission a masterpiece of 20th century modern architecture. All he knew was that he wanted a comfortable house with a 270-degree panoramic view built on his spectacular lot and that it had to be done within his budget. By the time the architect and the client got together, Stahl had interviewed a number of architects, all of whom were stymied by the site and considered it unbuildable. Located in a peripheral area of the Hollywood Hills at the summit of a mountain made of decomposed granite, the narrow and irregular strip of land had ragged edges that severely limited the dimensions of the level pad. The site's geotectonic demands were uncompromising and clearly incompatible with a conventional house. Stahl and his wife Charlotta had seen Koenig's radically radiant work in the

A skin of uninterrupted glass set into sliding door frames wraps the house in transparency.

ABOVE *Visible from Sunset Boulevard, 125 feet below, the steel structure seems to float in thin air.*
OPPOSITE *Pierre Koenig, FAIA*

Pictorial Living section of the *Los Angeles Examiner* in 1956;
this was the kind of alternative architecture they envisioned
on their sweeping promontory of rugged terrain.

Los Angeles in the 1950s, was a land of dreams, with
optimistic hopes for a future full of promise and economic
stability. The austerity of the war years was a fast-fading
memory. Open and free experimentation permeated all
of the mid-twentieth century art forms, imbuing them with
excitement and light. Modern music, modern painting and
modern architecture were finding their niche in a uniquely
neoteric time. Contemporary architecture had evolved
from the unrelenting austerity of the European Modernist
Movement of the 1920s and 1930s into the unrestrained
exuberance of a postwar, idealistic generation. Modern
architects were utilizing the basic Bauhaus principles to
explore the potential of a prefabricated and mass-produced
building system.

John Entenza's *Arts and Architecture* magazine had begun
the legendary Case Study program in 1945, and in 1956,
Pierre Koenig was invited to join the illustrious group of
architects, including Charles and Ray Eames, Eero Saarinen,
Raphael Soriano and Richard Neutra, who had already constructed Case Study houses. Designed to provide the average
American family with attractive and affordable housing that
would improve their everyday lifestyle, Entenza's ambitious
program encouraged his chosen few architects to allow themselves the freedom to create innovatively and without restric-
tion, using the newest postwar materials available in the
country. The magazine published and promoted the Case
Study houses and played a major role in advancing the concept and plausibility of the modern house as an industrial-
ized housing system that could be built more efficiently and
at costs equivalent to those of traditional homes. It was only
the fear and reluctance of the building industry and steel
companies to try new means of mass domestic construction
that kept the steel-frame house from the same post-war
proliferation as the more conventional tract house.

It was not until the early coverage of Case Study House
#21 in *Arts and Architecture* magazine and other publications
around the country that C.H. (Buck) Stahl got in touch
with Koenig, recognizing that the young architect's spare
and elegant steel constructions might solve the problems
of his difficult lot. Aptly named for the project to come
(*stahl* is German for steel), the former All-American football
star was aware that his parcel of land was best suited to
a contemporary house that offered panoramic views of
Los Angeles. Buck Stahl was a purchasing agent for
Lockheed Corporation's Engineering Department in the
San Fernando Valley and was an experienced shopper of
technical materials. He was a man professionally trained
in getting the most for his money. His high-in-the-sky real
estate was a definite bargain, but without the right architect,
it was just a costly mistake.

*Steel isn't something you can pick up and put down;
it is a way of life.*
PIERRE KOENIG

Pierre Koenig came home from the war in 1946 on the Queen Mary, sleeping in a lifeboat on deck for two weeks rather than participate in the abysmal living conditions provided below. Always the nonconformist, he chose the chilling air over the warmth of the troop ship's crowded quarters. In similar fashion, he has chosen a life path that has provided him the bracing, sometimes arctic atmosphere necessary to practice his art on his own terms.

Hoping for a college education, Koenig enlisted in the United States Army's Advanced Special Training Program, which offered volunteers a full four year curriculum abbreviated to two years. He had studied engineering at the University of Utah for only one semester when the program was cancelled, and the seventeen-year-old Koenig joined the ranks of GIs, attending the basic training program that prepared him not only for his Army experiences, but also in many ways for life. In Texas, he was trained to become a flash ranging observer, a skill which he used in frontline combat in France and Germany so effectively that he was not discharged from service until 1946.

Once home, Koenig renewed his efforts to achieve a college education, attending Pasadena City College on the GI Bill until he could gain admission to the University of Southern California. After a two year waiting period, he was finally accepted into the USC School of Architecture whose program was just beginning to shift emphasis from the classical Beaux Arts style to Modernism. Koenig was in his appropriate element. While a student at USC, he designed and built his first steel-framed house, using his Army discharge pay to buy a lot in Glendale and to finance the construction on a very thin shoestring. This was the house that caught the eye of John Entenza and later motivated him to ask Koenig to join the Case Study program.

'L'-shaped and spare, the futuristic wing of structural steel that was to become CSH #22 was assembled on site in a single September day in 1959. Prefabricated in the factory to Koenig's precise specifications, the steel sections were transported in an articulated truck up the steep and winding

Arts and Architecture *Magazine published an eight page layout of the completed Case Study House #22 in June, 1960*

Pierre Koenig taught me that math is music.
RONALD ALTOON, FAIA

roads to the client's location. Once there, the rectangular modules were assembled like a gigantic erector set under the architect's exacting eye. In a daring display of mathematical acumen, Koenig utilized only two structural components in designing the steel frame. Twelve-inch I-beams and four-inch H-columns were set twenty feet apart to create a grid of twenty-by-twenty bays, three along the short end of the L, and four defining the north-south axis. The underlying calculations of this minimalist equation contain within them a mysterious symmetry: I-beam + H-column = Elegance. Welded to the foundation and the reinforced concrete caissons that went deep into the granite below, the skeletal frame of the house cantilevered out ten feet into open space at the southeast corner of the property. The steel sculpture, visible from Sunset Boulevard 125 feet below, seemed to be dangling in thin air, yet Los Angeles' most representational image had literally been set in stone.

Nine months later in June of 1960, *Arts and Architecture* magazine published an eight-page layout of the completed CSH #22, featuring extraordinary photographs by Julius Shulman and explanatory text by Pierre Koenig. The architect describes it as a pavillion-type house in an ideal setting and walks the reader through his construction explaining the details along the way. A skin of uninterrupted glass set into sliding-door frames wraps the house in transparency, unbroken except for a solid curtain wall of short span steel decking to provide privacy at the street entrance. Soaring over the house is the spectacular long span roof decking that cantilevers eight feet out over the inner courtyard providing shade for the house's interiors and shelter for the recreational pool area. The house and the swimming pool are integral to each other and are bound together by a series of concrete terraces and walks.

The house interior is divided into the living area and the sleeping area along the lines of the "L" and at its juncture is the guest bath, master bath, service porch and walk-in dressing room. Adjoining this in the short wing is the master bedroom suite, and the children's two bedrooms, each with private bath and divided by a folding partition. The long wing of the house is 70 feet of space surrounded by glass, and at the center of the living room, a raised stone hearth supports a free-standing fireplace that is framed with 4-inch steel angles and open on all sides. The steel-framed furniture lends another architectural component to the atmosphere of the house. The kitchen is at the far end of the living area, separated by a low wall of kitchen cabinets containing two stainless steel sinks. The range top, two ovens, refrigerator, and washer and dryer are all electric. All of the rooms open onto the swimming pool and recreational areas, creating a fusion between inside and outside that reflects Koenig's life-long commitment to environmentally-oriented architecture.

Director of the Natural Forces Laboratory at the University of Southern California where he was recently made a Distinguished Professor, Koenig advises his students to build in tune with nature, using to full advantage passive-ventilation (or heating and cooling) systems that are ultimately more reliable than mechanical systems. Because each job site has its own micro-climate, he recommends careful study of all of its aspects before beginning the design process, the same procedure he followed with CSH #22. Utilizing the benign aspects of the Southern California climate, he calculated the heat of the sun in different seasons and the flow of the site's prevailing breezes to determine the environmental plan. The solar panels that provide radiant heating for the swimming pool are an example of his early awareness. Because the panels were not commercially available in 1959, Koenig had them built on the site, fabricating wood-frame boxes that held coiled water pipes covered with fiberglass panels. He also used radiant heating for the house itself, installing the system of gas-heated coils on the ground before the slab was poured. Because of his environmentally sound design principles, none of Koenig's Southern California houses require air-conditioning, and CSH #22 was no exception. The Stahls have learned to operate their openable walls of glass like flaps on a flying wing, expertly capturing the wind whenever they need it.

96   Buck and Charlotta Stahl have lived in their famous
house, one of the most photographed in the world, for close
to four decades; its fortieth birthday takes place during the
year 2000. There, they have raised their family and when the
children grew up and moved away, the Stahls built themselves a new and interesting life in the film industry. Over
the years, csh #22 has gained status as a favored location for
numerous movies, television and print ads, appearing ubiq-
uitously in the background of films with a Los Angeles
setting such as "The Marrying Kind" with Alec Baldwin,
"Playing By Heart" with Sean Connery, and Robert De
Niro's "Heat." The Stahls can watch the production process
unfold in their living room, or they have the option to
move, all expenses paid, to a nearby luxury hotel if the film-
ing becomes too lengthy. As a result, their home has become
a source of ongoing entertainment while providing them
with a considerable annual income.

    In 1989, the Los Angeles Museum of Contemporary
Art (moca) used the Frank Gehry-designed Temporary
Contemporary facility for an exhibition titled "Blueprints
For Modern Living." An indepth examination of the Case
Study program, the highly successful presentation curated by
Elizabeth Smith with installation by Craig Hodgetts and
Ming Fung, featured a full-scale three-dimensional replica of
Koenig's csh #22. The program was open to the public for
five months during which thousands of visitors had the
opportunity to walk through the authentically furnished
model and experience it firsthand.

    Both of Pierre Koenig's Case Study Houses, #21 and
#22, were approved for Historical Cultural Monument
status by the Los Angeles Conservancy and were designated
in November 1999. Koenig himself was awarded the
American Institute of Architects/Los Angeles Gold Medal
in October, 1999.

The futuristic wing of structural steel was assembled on site in a single day.

THE GETTY CENTER

"In Los Angeles, the light seems to reach every corner of the landscape; when I first visited the site of the future Getty Center, on a beautiful day with unusually good visibility, I immediately understood that light and space were central to the California experience."

Richard Meier,
BUILDING THE GETTY

Wrapped in the antiquity of ancient stone, the heterogenous group of Modernist buildings situated on the massive campus of the Getty Center Complex seem like a citadel from another time. Rough surfaces of golden travertine appear everywhere, on the buildings, on the walls, underfoot as paving, as jagged benches of sculptural form, and in beautiful uncut stones embedded with fossils placed at eye level within the regular grid of the walls. Mined from a quarry at Bagni di Tivoli just north of Rome, the travertine is the unifying force of the collage of complex elements that form Richard Meier's museum complex, grounding them into their natural setting in the rugged terrain of the Santa Monica Mountains.

The stone slabs were produced by an automated "guillotine" system devised specifically for the Getty Center project

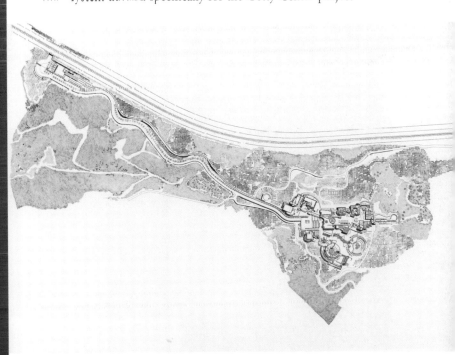

Site Plan of the Getty Center

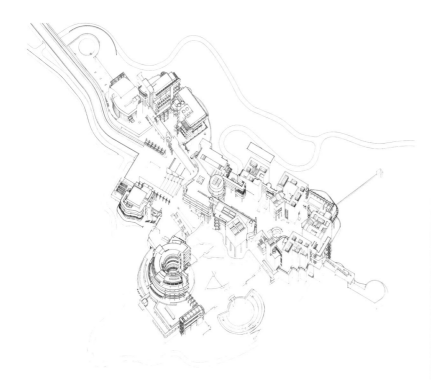

by Richard Meier and quarry owner Carlo Mariotti after a year of experimentation. A mechanical device with a falling blade split the chunks of travertine down the center along their fault lines. Natural physics determined their size of two-feet six-inches; anything larger was splintered by the cutting edge. Meier's vision for cladding large sections of the exterior walls with these cleft stones was based on an open-joint panel system he had developed in Europe which aligned them precisely without the use of mortar. Over 150 different types of 'clips' were invented to fasten the travertine to the varied tectonic applications throughout the Getty complex, applying it to skeleton steel frames and concrete walls with equal success. Although the retaining walls and the bases of all the buildings are faced with stone, the upper stories and curvilinear elements of the structures are clad in off-white enameled metal panels that soar upward from the travertine as though connecting earth and sky.

In 1982, the Getty Oil stock that J. Paul Getty bequeathed to the museum upon his death became a $700 million dollar endowment, a sum that increased dramatically to $1.7 billion when Texaco acquired Getty Oil a year later. Under the leadership of new president Harold M. Williams, a past chairman of the U.S. Securities Commission, the Getty Trust purchased 742 acres in Brentwood. Planning to preserve most of it against future development, 24 acres of the hilltop site has been used for the museum and ancillary facilities, establishing a major cultural institution for art and related research in museum management, education, conservation and art history. The Trust wanted to expand the cultural legacy of J. Paul Getty beyond the guidelines he had established for his museum in Malibu with its collection of European paintings, Greek and Roman antiquities and 18th century French decorative art. The Malibu museum is a replica of the Villa dei Papiri, a Roman villa buried under the debris of an eruption of Mount Vesuvius in A.D. 79, a classical reproduction on an intimate scale that overlooks the Pacific Ocean. The Getty Trust's new hilltop site in Brentwood offered a sweeping view of the ocean and the

entire city of Los Angeles, and the trustees envisioned a
world-class art center and museum complex built into its
rugged terrain. The ambitious project required an architect
with sensibilities that matched their own, and the Trust
appointed a search committee to begin the painstaking
process of finding the right person for the job.

The selection process began in 1983, when thirty-three
internationally known architects were invited to submit cre-
dentials and materials to the search committee for consideration. On November 23rd of that year, Richard Meier was
notified that he was being considered along with six other
candidates. Early in 1984, Meier toured his major projects
with the selection committee, visiting the High Museum
in Atlanta, the Atheneum in New Harmony, and the
Museum for Decorative Arts in Frankfurt. On April 23rd, he
was informed that he was on the final shortlist with British
architect James Stirling and Fumihiko Maki from Japan.
On October 26, 1984, he received a phone call and follow-up
confirmation telegram from Harold Williams appointing
him as the Getty Center architect.

At the age of sixteen, Richard Meier went to work as a
"gofer" in a small New Jersey architectural firm owned by a
family friend. The son of affluent Jewish parents, Meier was
far too interested in art and architecture to seriously consider
going into the thriving family tanning business, and in 1952,
enrolled at Cornell University, taking courses in painting, art
history and architecture. Soon after his graduation in 1957,
he went to Europe, visiting Israel, Greece, Italy, France and
Germany. He returned to New York after six months and
took a position with Skidmore, Owings and Merrill, a firm
he credits with teaching him the inner workings of a corpo-
rate office. His next job was with Marcel Breuer, where he
was an apprentice for three years, and in the following years
he began a series of small commissions, including a house
for his parents in Essex Fells, New Jersey. His reputation
as an abstract modernist, known as the "white architect,"
began with the Smith House in Darien, Connecticut and
continued throughout his distinguished career as he gained

Richard Meier, FAIA

increasingly prestigious commissions in both Europe and
America. In May 1984, while still awaiting word from the
Getty selection committee, Meier was awarded the Pritzker
Architecture Prize.

When the architect first walked the sunlit site of his
colossal new commission, he was struck with the energy of
its undulating topography. Covered with native chaparral
and teeming with indigenous wildlife, the natural beauty of
the Brentwood hilltop sloped gently on the west to meet the
built environment of luxurious homes, and more sharply on
the eastern edge toward the perpetual drone of traffic from
the San Diego Freeway and the Sepulveda Pass. From a
promontory at the southernmost end of the landform, the
spectacular 360-degree view swept from the distant buildings
of downtown Los Angeles to the vast panorama of the Pacific
Ocean, with the beach cities of Southern California to the
south and the San Fernando Valley to the north. Two ridges
outlined the building site, one lining up along the Los

Angeles street grid and the other parallel to the north-south path of the San Diego Freeway at the bottom of the hill. Nine hundred feet above sea level and four hundred feet above the plane below, the mountain that the Getty Trust had purchased would soon become the largest single-phase construction project in the history of the city of Los Angeles. Preparation of the Getty site began in September 1987, and it would take years of raging controversy and contentious discussion between the Trustees, the various Getty committees, the Brentwood Homeowner's Association, the Los Angeles Planning Commission and Richard Meier's office before the monumental architectural complex was finally completed.

The tram is white; a series of connecting cars that Richard Meier called "a kind of automatic, horizontal elevator" to transport visitors up the hill to the Getty Center. Cable-drawn and air-cushion supported, the tram makes the serpentine ascent in less than five minutes; a silent, non-polluting form of transit that provides ever-changing views of Los Angeles and the freeway below and the landscaping and buildings emerging above. The tram pulls up at a small canopy-covered station, with travertine paving that leads to the Arrival Plaza and a wide stone stairway. At the top of the stairs is the axial three-story Rotunda with its great curved glass doors that open to the promenade of the Museum Courtyard and the spatial depth of the inviting tree-lined scenery beyond. The circular top-lit foyer of the Rotunda is a hub of activity, the center of the great exhilarating storm of art and architecture taking place on the deconstructed hilltop of the Santa Monica Mountains.

The ground plan of the Museum, the primary visitor destination, is a grouping of two-story pavilions situated around a central courtyard. The series of pavilion clusters are linked together by covered walkways, corridors and terraces, all of which frame spectacular views of the world outside. Each has an adjacent stairway and elevator between the two floors of galleries. A clockwise route through the galleries offers a chronological sequence of art from the manuscripts,

sculptures and ceramics of the Middle Ages and the Renaissance to the photography of the twentieth century. The lower levels contain the decorative art rooms, and a curved staircase in the Rotunda leads to a succession of painting galleries on the upper levels. Each of the pavilions is devoted to a specific period of art—the North Pavilion to the left of the Rotunda features pre-1600 art and classical sculpture; the East Pavilion art is from 1600 to 1800; and art dating from after 1800 can be found at the southern end of the courtyard in the West Pavilion. A large gallery for temporary exhibitions is located to the right of the Rotunda.

The gallery atriums on the Museum's upper levels, where the paintings are on display, are fitted with neutral tinted glass and meet the conservation limits of 35% transmittance. Based on the movable louver system of the skylights at the Dulwich Picture Gallery in London, the overhead louvers have been programmed to exclude direct sun and adapt to outside conditions, filtering the natural light to appropriate levels in the galleries throughout the day. Around the base of the skylight is a recessed border containing supplementary artificial light. The lower level galleries, with collections of decorative arts, drawings, manuscripts and photographs, require lower levels of light and are equipped with clerestory windows and artificial lighting, both systems adjustable for reasons of preservation.

The design of the gallery interiors was done by the office of Richard Meier with participation from New York architect and interior designer, Thierry Despont. In association with Meier, Despont, whose celebrity clientele includes Bill Gates and Ralph Lauren, designed the elaborate enclave of fourteen galleries within the Museum; a succession of period rooms that follows the evolving styles of French decorative arts and furniture from the late seventeenth through the late eighteenth centuries.

In addition to the Museum, which is situated at the southeast corner of the hilltop property, there are five component buildings set along the Y-shaped periphery of the 24-acre site. In response to height restrictions, over half the

*"Sometimes I think that the landscape overtakes it, and
sometimes I see the structure as standing out, dominating
the landscape. The two are entwined in a dialogue,
a perpetual embrace in which building and site are one."*
BUILDING THE GETTY, Richard Meier

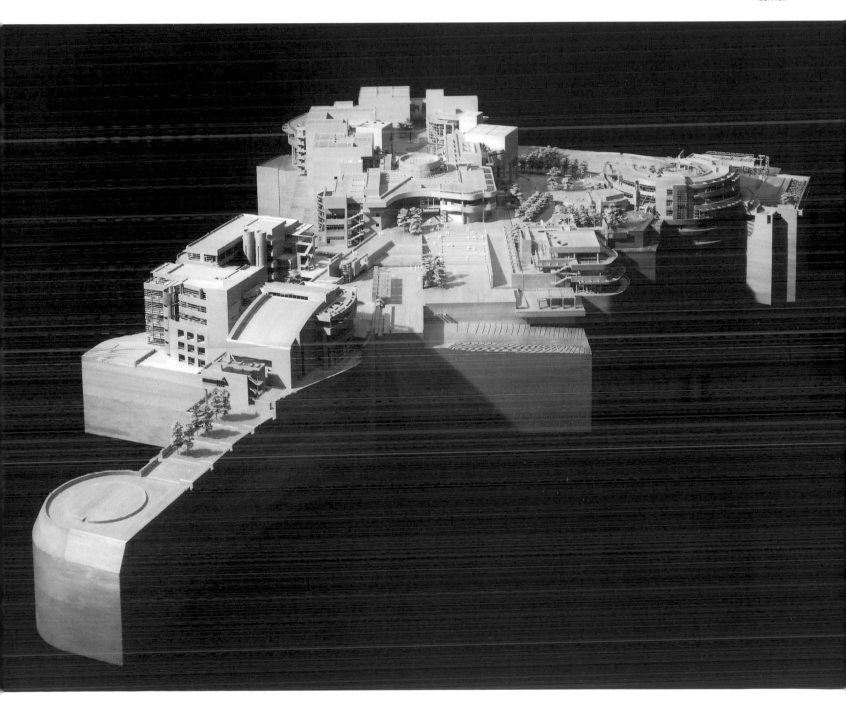

Getty Center model

space of the Getty Center Complex on the east and south sides is placed into the excavated hill below ground level Most buildings are designed with three stories above ground and three stories below, and all are linked together with subterranean corridors at a common level. The eastern ridge of the property, with a height limit of 65 feet, presents a bold site profile of travertine-clad buildings rising from the terrain: the Auditorium; the Museum; the North Building, housing the J. Paul Getty Trust and the Information Institute; and the East Building, comprised of the Conservation Institute, Education Institute and the Grant Program. The Research Institute for the History of Art and the Humanities overlooks the residential neighborhood on the western ridge of the property in response to its more stringent height limit of 45 feet.

Rising from the wild natural terrain of the Santa Monica mountain range on which the Getty Center is situated is the beginning of a remarkable synthesis between architecture and landscape, a vast carpet of 8,500 native oak trees planted on the slopes that merges seamlessly into the surrounding vegetation. The geometric grid of trees is underplanted with fire retardant ground cover that also provides erosion protection and storm water control. The transition from the planted forest of oaks, to the Getty's outer fringe to the landscaping of the entire hilltop enclave is equally subtle; an interrelated spatial scheme that coalesces the categories of structure, pavilion, terrace, garden and water feature in a coherent and beautiful design. Planned by the Richard Meier office in collaboration with successive landscape architects Emmet Wemple, Dan Kiley and the Olin Partnership, the collective design has the ambience of a Renaissance Italian villa garden that has somehow been transported over space and time into a new idyllic setting of golden Los Angeles light. The Central Garden, set into the natural ravine between the Museum and the Research Institute, is a spectacular outdoor art installation by Southern California artist

Robert Irwin, who called the work "a sculpture in the form of a garden aspiring to be art." Chiseling natural elements to fit into his vision for the garden, Irwin designed a sinuous watercourse that cascades over a granite wall into an elaborate formation of terraced beds centered with a large pool below. A walk designed to accommodate the disabled leads over a small stream to a terrace featuring bougainvillea trained into trees on metal forms. The circular pool is filled with a spiraling maze of precisely clipped azalea bushes that appear to float on its surface.

The J. Paul Getty Trust is a private philanthropic foundation that creates and supervises its own programs in the arts and the humanities. It is legally required to spend a certain percentage of its endowment each year and has done so in a manner that has been a unique gift to the people of Los Angeles. The unprecedented success of the Getty Center Complex can be attributed to many factors, the most striking of which is the ongoing celebration of life, art and architecture to be found at the top of the hill. Thousands of visitors a day have come to enjoy the veritable feast of pleasures offered to the general public, many of them coming back on a regular basis to stroll through the gardens, visit the galleries, attend a performance or admire the myriad views so elegantly framed within the Getty's architecture.

The circular, top-lit entry hall

DISNEY CONCERT HALL

It is unusual for a building to achieve status as an icon before it is built, but the Disney Concert Hall has occupied the center of attention since it left the drawing board. Beginning construction 10 years after it was designed, the stainless steel 'sails' of Frank O. Gehry's concert hall embody the spirit, exuberance and place that is Los Angeles.

Lillian Disney, a leading Los Angeles philanthropist, wanting to honor her late husband Walt Disney, donated fifty million dollars in 1987 for a new concert hall for the Los Angeles Philharmonic Orchestra. It was to be part of the Music Center complex in the city block bounded by Grand Avenue, First Street, Hope Street and Second Street, on historic Bunker Hill in the heart of Downtown Los Angeles. An architectural search committee was formed to set up an invitational competition for the building's design. After visiting concert halls in the United States and Europe, the committee of members including Richard Koshalek, Director of the Los Angeles Museum of Contemporary Art (MOCA); Ernest Fleischmann, Director of the Los Angeles Philharmonic; Lillian Disney, and others of the Los Angeles cultural elite, narrowed the selection to four candidates: James Stirling, Gottfried Bohm, Hans Hollein, and Frank Gehry.

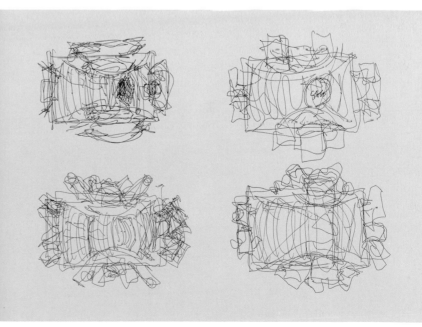

Gehry's Picasso-like sketches of the Concert Hall

108

The Philharmonic had issued a preliminary guide informing contestants of the three fundamental objectives of the design competition: to focus on acoustical excellence and on uniting the orchestra and the audience; to create a socially responsible building open and available to the people of Los Angeles that reflected its culture and diversity; and to integrate the new building with the Music Center and its existing surroundings. Lillian Disney added a request that extensive gardens be included in the design. Given these parameters, Frank Gehry created his "music barge," a great, swooping conglomeration of sculptural shapes and sizes that focused on the excellence of its acoustics, had an entrance foyer with gardens open daily to the public, and was built on a configuration that linked it to the Music Center and to MOCA.

Richard Koshalek, chairman of the committee, thought it by far the strongest entry and recommended its approval. Ernest Fleischmann was impressed with the informed acoustical systems, and Lillian Disney was enchanted with the whole concept and its numerous gardens. As a result, in December 1988, Frank Gehry was chosen as the architect of the new Disney Concert Hall. What followed was an odyssey of anguish something like Hemingway's *Old Man And The Sea*, with Gehry's monumental fish, his design for the Concert Hall, being nibbled into nothing by a sea of dissent and controversy. He has fought his battles well, and the design as it exists today is the uncompromising result of his intractable resolve to adhere to his inner vision of a ship you can board and listen to music.

When Frank Gehry was 51 years old, he decided to close his thriving office in Brentwood and start all over again. He had just completed two milestone projects crucial to his career; Santa Monica Place, a shopping center that broke the mold, and his own famous Westside residence which was instantly reviled and even stoned by irate neighbors. On the night Santa Monica Place opened, he invited the developer to his home for dinner. Sitting around the table in a celebratory mood, the developer suddenly asked the architect which project he had the most fun doing, the shopping center or the extensive renovation of his house. For Gehry, it was a no-brainer: the house won hands down. It was all his, with no compromises and concessions to be made, a free, creative statement enjoined upon what he calls his 'dumb little house.' Realizing he was at a crossroads, Gehry took the first step toward the kind of professional freedom he craved, signing off from the next project that he and the Santa Monica Place developer had planned together. He reopened his office in a small storefront space on Ocean Front Walk in Venice Beach within a month and reduced his staff from thirty to three.

The Gehry house in Santa Monica was originally a sedate, two-story Dutch Colonial painted pink. Located on a quiet street in a distinctly middle class neighborhood, the traditional house was small and unpretentious and within a price range Gehry and his wife Berta could afford. They had been living with their two young sons in a cramped apartment, and it was Gehry's mother who persuaded them to move. Although it was the antithesis of his philosophy of architecture, Gehry felt an affection for the little house that Berta had found and determined to transform it, not destroy it. He wanted to build a house around a house, so as to allow the original to maintain its own integrity as the renovating materials wrapped it in modernity. It was the architect's unorthodox choice of industrial materials that caused the house's notoriety, an uninhibited juxtaposition of chain-link fencing, corrugated metal, plywood and asphalt flooring that had the neighbors agape and astounded. Gehry had studied the neighborhood when they first moved in, noticing the boat in one backyard and cars on blocks in others. The industrial materials were there, only in a different form from what he chose. But from the homeowners' point of view, their real estate values were being endangered by Gehry's glitzy exhibitionism, and they were up in arms. As it turned out, his famous house not only enhanced the neighborhood's worth, but the street became a de rigeur visit for architecture buffs from all over the world.

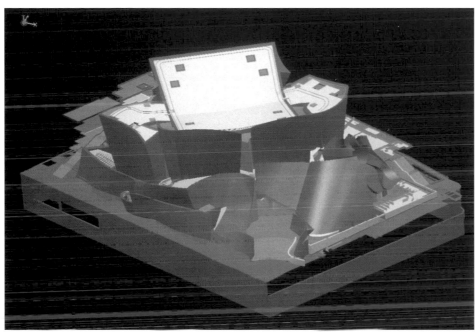

LEFT   *CATIA models*
ABOVE   *Frank O. Gehry, FAIA*

OVERLEAF   *Hall study models*

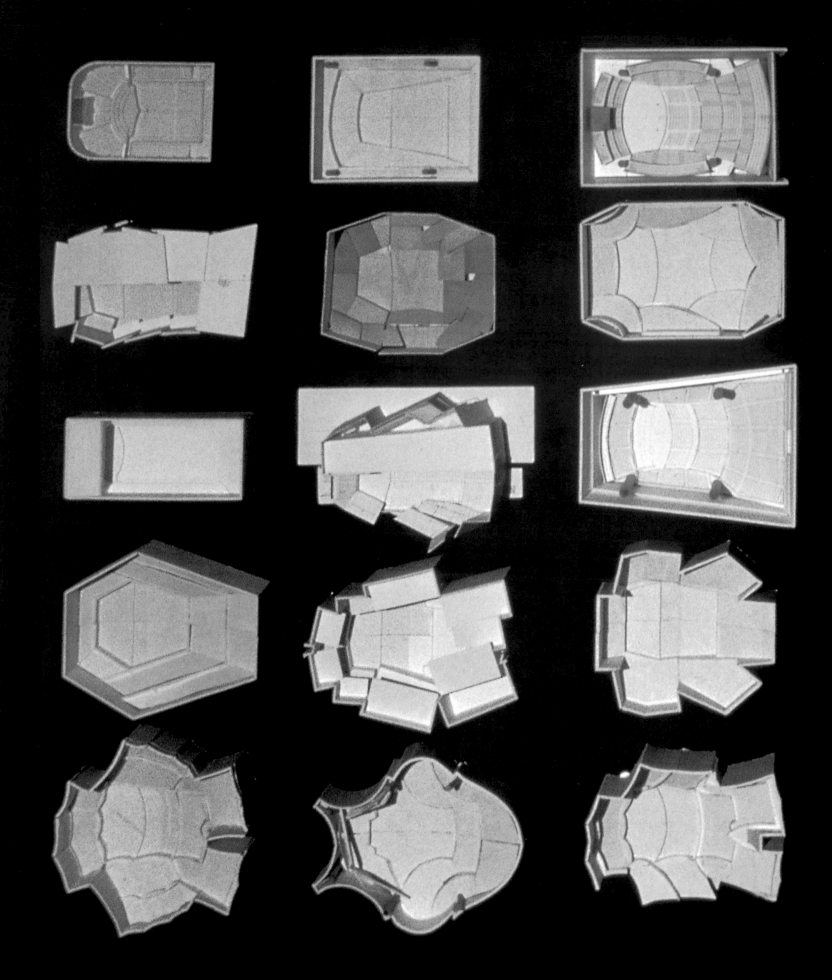

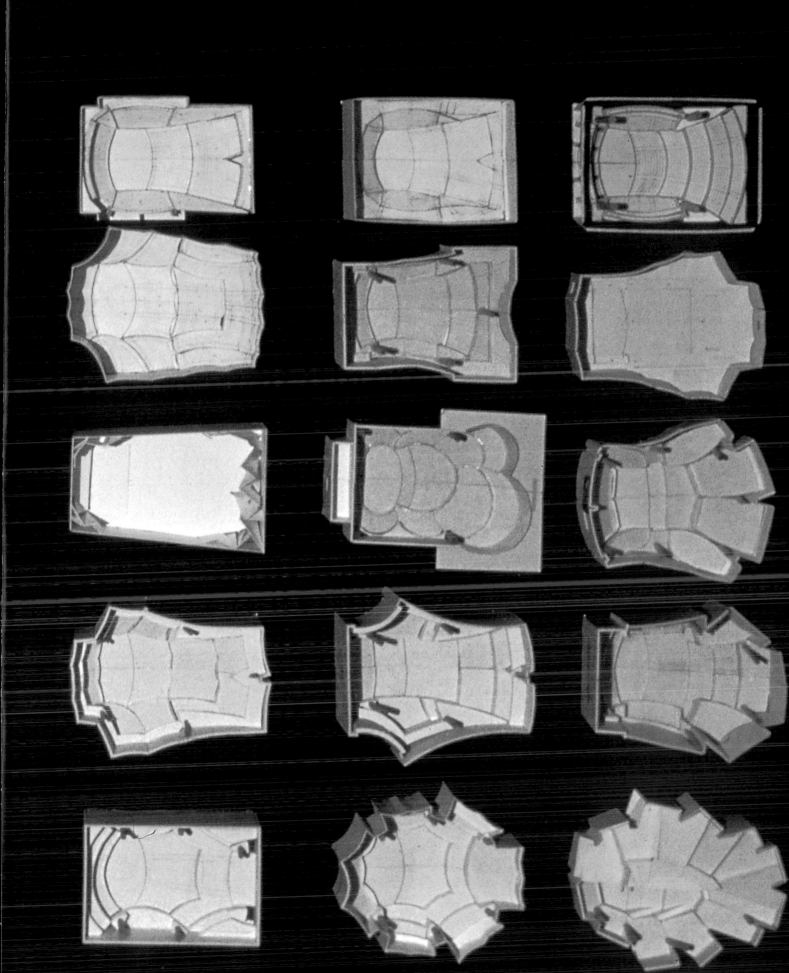

112

Final design model

Gehry's drawings have evolved, along with his philosophy of architecture, from the classical renderings he learned at school to the Picasso-like shorthand of wobbly power lines with which, he says, he tries to find the building within the paper. Always exhilarated by art, he has surrounded himself since early in his career with avant-garde LA artists such as Ed Moses, Larry Bell, Billy Al Bengston and Chuck Arnoldi. He designed a line of cardboard furniture called Easy Edges with Bill Irwin and collaborated on architectural projects with Frank Stella and Richard Serra. The gargantuan binoculars on the street facade of his Chiat/Day/Mojo headquarters in Venice are the work of friends Claes Oldenburg and Coosje van Bruggen.

The years between the move to the Venice office and the commission for the Disney Concert Hall were challenging and inventive. The tiny office space was crammed with

models brought from his larger quarters, and Gehry began work on new ones for such projects as the Norton House, the Indiana Home Studios and Rebecca's Restaurant, all in Venice. The funky atmosphere of Ocean Front Walk and its primitive patina of sand, sun and water was a suitable background for the architect's productive creativity, as was the companionship of the lively group of artist friends who lived in the neighborhood.

He sought major commissions in Europe, and built the Vitra International Furniture Manufacturing Facility and Design Museum and the American Center in Paris. Finally, in 1987, he achieved his first major commission in Los Angeles, winning the invitational competition for the Disney Concert Hall. The history of the building and the history of the controversy surrounding it are tenaciously intertwined and now a part of the city's lore. Gehry's winning entry

became a political football and was subject to endless wrangling and censure. Over the years, it has been dissected and transmogrified by all of the players involved. At one point, Gehry walked away from the project and told them to get another architect but was persuaded to come back. The concert hall went through so many changes and adjustments that Gehry had 60 models of its variations to show at the 1996 Biennale in Venice, Italy.

In Gehry's original plan and in all of its eventual permutations, the configuration of the building was determined by the acoustic parameters. He had studied the inexact science of acoustics thoroughly before he designed his successful installation of fiberglass spheres at the Hollywood Bowl, and he understood its power in a building that was meant to contain music. Planning his entry for the concert hall competition, Gehry used the guidelines for acoustics suggested

by the architectural search committee. They recommended the ideas of an acoustical expert from France, leading the Gehry team to design separate 'shoebox' spaces in the auditorium's interior. After he won the competition, a group from the Philharmonic was formed to learn more about the current state of sound systems, visiting the Boston Symphony, The Amsterdam Concertgebow, the Berlin Philharmonic and Tokyo's Suntory Hall. Using the new information they garnered, a scale model of each venue was constructed and studied by Gehry's office. Minoru Nagata, Suntory Hall's acoustician, was brought in for consultation on the final design. His theory was that convex surfaces distribute sound, and that the building's interior walls should follow the upward path of the music. After discussing Nagata's suggestions with musicians and conductors including Esa-Pekka Salonen, Pierre Boulez, Zubin Mehta and

Final design model of the Concert Hall interior

"I think of it as a music barge, some kind of ship with a canopy which you can board to listen to music. The barge is made out of wood with flying sails, which works well visually, but in fact the material and the shapes are of acoustic importance."
FRANK O. GEHRY, Academy Press, Frank Gehry

Simon Rattle, Gehry combined the ideas of the two schools of acoustics and opened his interior spaces to more closely follow the contours of organic form.

The interior changes determined the exterior changes, and the architectural sculpture on Bunker Hill was molded and tweaked into a compatible aesthetic. Within the crevices of the two skins, the architect fitted a cafe, terraces, gardens and the Founders Room. Inside the 2,290-seat concert hall, wooden seating blocks of Douglas Fir will surround the orchestra platform, a seating arrangement reminiscent of Shakespeare's Old Globe Theater. In a central position between seating blocks and the rear of the stage is a pipe organ designed to augment the interior's ambience. Natural light will flow into the hall through skylights and a large window at the back of the auditorium, subtly illuminating daytime concerts. Wood walls and the sails of the wooden ceiling enhance Gehry's seagoing analogy.

Located in the center of its square block site, the Concert Hall will be surrounded by an urban oasis of extensive gardens that will relate it to the existing Music Center and will perform the function of public accessibility from adjacent streets. A private garden for musicians will be available in the backstage technical area. The entry plaza at the corner of First and Grand, and a secondary entry plaza at Second and Grand, will be invitations to passersby to come into the complex and enjoy the numerous amenities including a gift shop, a restaurant and cafe. Two outdoor amphitheaters and a pre-concert performance space will offer educational programs, lectures and small-scale presentations that will encourage interaction between artists and visitors. The Concert Hall lobby, faced with a curtain wall of large, operable glass panels, will be open to the public throughout the day.

The California Institute of the Arts will have its own facility, the Roy and Edna Disney/CalArts multi-use black-box theater, in the base of the building where it will have direct street access from Hope and Second Streets. The Theater has its own lobby, art gallery and cafe, and will be CalArts' major venue in the city of Los Angeles. A six-level 2,500-car underground garage, with a cascade of escalators featuring alternating art installations, will be located below the Concert Hall with access from three surrounding streets.

Titanium and stainless steel cladding were under consideration for the exterior of the building, the choice depending on the availability of materials at the time of construction. Titanium is a natural element used today in aircraft landing gear and in sporting equipment such as tennis racquets and golf clubs. Frank Gehry pioneered its architectural application in Bilbao, Spain, creating his mammoth shimmering art form with a museum inside. By the time of the December 1999 groundbreaking ceremony, Gehry had made his decision, choosing stainless steel cladding. Reiterating his deeply felt music barge analogy, he says he wants the material to be reflective enough in the California daylight to "go almost white, like white sails." When the Disney Concert Hall is completed, sometime around the 2002–2003 Philharmonic season, the architect will have made another incandescent masterpiece, this time for his hometown, the city of Los Angeles.

BIBLIOGRAPHY

SOURCES

Scott, Allen J. and Soja, Edward W. *The City: Los Angeles and Urban Theory at the End of the Twentieth Century*. Berkeley: University of California Press, 1996.

Jodidio, Philip. *Contemporary California Architecture*. Switzerland: Taschen, 1991.

Johnson, Paul C. (Ed.). *Los Angeles: Portrait of an Extraordinary City*. Menlo Park: Lane Magazine and Book Company, 1968.

Walker, Derek (Guest Ed.). *Los Angeles: Architecture Design Profile*. St. Martin's Press, Academy Editions.

Kaplan, Sam Hall. *LA Lost and Found: An Architectural History of Los Angeles*. New York: Crown Publishers, Inc., 1987.

Starr, Kevin. *Inventing the Dream: California Through the Progressive Era*. New York: Oxford University Press, 1985.

LIBRARIES AND COLLECTIONS

UCLA Research Library, University of California at Los Angeles
Los Angeles Central Library
Edward L. Doheny, Jr. Library, University of Southern California
Architecture and Fine Arts Library, University of Southern California
Santa Monica Library, California Special Collections
Security Pacific National Bank Collection, Los Angeles
Los Angeles Conservancy Archives

INTERVIEWS

Thomas Buckley, Tracy Lyon, Ira Yellin, Julius Shulman, Jane Summer, Kevin Feeney, Kathy Towell, Francis J. Weber, Nancy Lopez, Dr. E.C. Krupp, Kara Knack, Marvin Rand, Karen Hudson, Charlotta and Buck Stahl, Pierre Koenig, Michael Palladino, Frank O. Gehry, Keith Mendenhall

CHAPTER 1: MISSION SAN FERNANDO REY DE ESPAÑA

Krell, Dorothy (Chief Editor). *The California Missions: A Pictorial History by the Sunset Editors*. Menlo Park: Lane Publishing Company, 1979.

Engelhardt, Fr. Zephyrin. *San Fernando Rey: The Mission of the Valley*. Ramona: Ballena Press, 1927.

Weber, Francis J. (compiled and edited by). *The Mission in the Valley: A Documentary History of San Fernando Rey de España*. Libra Press, 1975.

Nunis, Doyce B., Jr. (Ed.) *Mission San Fernando Rey de España: A Bicentennial Tribute*. Historical Society of Southern California.

CHAPTER 2: THE BRADBURY BUILDING

McCoy, Esther. "A Vast Hall Full of Light," *Arts & Architecture* Magazine, 1953.

Herbert, Ray. "Grande Dame of Broadway," *Cry California*, Summer, 1967.

Reinhold, Robert. "New Life for a Neglected Jewel in Los Angeles," *The New York Times*, Sept. 25, 1991.

Groves, Martha. "A Vision for LA's Broadway," *Los Angeles Times*, Feb. 27, 1989.

CHAPTER 3: HOLLYHOCK HOUSE

Wright, Frank Lloyd. *An Autobiography: Frank Lloyd Wright*. New York: Horizon Press, 1977.

Hoffman, Donald. *Frank Lloyd Wright's Hollyhock House*. New York: Dover, 1992.

Steele, James. *Barnsdall House: Frank Lloyd Wright*.

Smith, Kathryn. *Frank Lloyd Wright, Hollyhock House and Olive Hill*. New York: Rizzoli, 1992.

Simo, Melanie. "Barnsdall Park: A New Master Plan for Frank Lloyd Wright's California Romanza." *01 Landmarks*. Washington DC: Spacemaker Press, 1997.

CHAPTER 4: WATTS TOWERS

Banham, Reyner. *Los Angeles: The Architecture of Four Ecologies*. New York: Harper & Row, 1971.

Whiteson, Leon. *Watts Towers of Los Angeles*. Oakville: Mosaic Press, 1989.

Goldstone, Bud and Goldstone, Arloa Paquin. *The Los Angeles Watts Towers*. Los Angeles: Getty Conservation Institute, 1997.

Zelver, Patricia. *The Wonderful Towers of Watts*. New York: Tambourine Books, 1994.

Watts Towers Committee. "Watts Towers." *California Special Collections*, 1959. Santa Monica Public Library.

Trillin, Calvin. "A Reporter at Large." *The New Yorker* Magazine, May 29, 1965.

CHAPTER 5: HOLLYWOOD BOWL

Northcutt, John Orlando. *Magic Valley: Story of the Hollywood Bowl*. Los Angeles: Osherenik Co., 1967.

Buckland, Michael and Henken, John (edited by). *The Hollywood Bowl: Tales of Summer Nights*. Los Angeles: Balcony Press, 1996.

Hollywood Bowl Catalogue, 1954. *California Special Collections*, Santa Monica Public Library.

CHAPTER 6: LOS ANGELES CITY HALL

Hales, George P. *Los Angeles City Hall*. Los Angeles: Times Mirror, 1928.

Gleye, Paul. *The Architecture of Los Angeles*. Los Angeles: Rosebud Books, 1981.

Fogelson, Robert M. *The Fragmented Metropolis*. Cambridge: Harvard University Press, 1967.

Project Restore. *City Hall: The Building*

Project Restore. *Los Angeles City Hall*

CHAPTER 7: GRAUMAN'S CHINESE THEATRE

Berger, Robert and Conser, Anne. *The Last Remaining Seats: Movie Palaces of Tinseltown*. Los Angeles: Balcony Press, 1997.

Naylor, David. *American Picture Palaces: The Architecture of Fantasy*. New York: Van Nostrand, 1981.

Endres, Stacey and Cushman, Robert. *Hollywood at Your Feet*. Los Angeles: Pomegranate Press, 1992.

Valentine, Maggie. *The Show Starts on the Sidewalk: An Architectural History of the Movie Theatre, starring S. Charles Lee*. New Haven: Yale University Press, 1994.

Beardsley, Charles. *Hollywood's Master Showman: The Legendary Sid Grauman*. Rosemont, 1983.

CHAPTER 8: GRIFFITH OBSERVATORY

Eberts, Mike. *Griffith Park: A Centennial History*. Los Angeles: Historical Society of Southern California, 1996.

Newmark, Harris. *Sixty Years in Southern California, 1853–1913*. Edited by Maurice H. and Marco R. Newmark. New York: Knickerbocker Press, 1916.

St John, Adela Rogers. *Final Verdict*. New York: Double Day, 1962.

Alter, Dinsmore. "Twenty Three Years of the Griffith Observatory," *Griffith Observer*, April 1958.

Whitnall, Gordon. "The Founding of Griffith Observatory," *Griffith Observer*, May 1960.

Bunton, George W. "Reminiscences of Early Times," *Griffith Observer*, May 1972.

"A Gift to the People of Los Angeles," *Griffith Park Quarterly*, January 1978.

Cook, Anthony. "The Secret History of Griffith Observatory," *Griffith Observer*, May 1994.

CHAPTER 9: UNION STATION

Gebhard, David and Winter, Robert. *Architecture in Los Angeles: A Compleat Guide*. Salt Lake City: Gibbs M. Smith, Inc., 1985.

Bradley, Bill. *The Last of the Great Stations: 40 Years of the Los Angeles Union Passenger Terminal*. Burbank: Interurban Publications, 1979.

Pitt, Leonard and Pitt, Dale. *Los Angeles A to Z: An Encyclopedia of the City and County*. Berkeley: University of California Press, 1997.

CHAPTER 10: CASE STUDY HOUSE 22

Steele, James and Jenkins, David. *Pierre Koenig*. London: Phaidon, 1998.

Smith, Elizabeth A.T.(Ed). *Blueprints for Modern Living: History and Legacy of the Case Study Houses*. Los Angeles: Museum of Contemporary Art/MIT Press, 1989.

Jackson, Lesley. *Contemporary*. London: Phaidon, 1995.

Jackson, Neil. "Another Splash," *RIBA Journal*, November 1994.

118

Giovannini, Joseph. "Study in Steel," *Elle Decor*, 1996.

Arts & Architecture Magazine, "Progress Report: Case Study House #22, Pierre Koenig," February 1960.

Arts & Architecture Magazine, "Completion: Case Study House #22, Pierre Koenig," June 1960.

CHAPTER 11: LAX THEME BUILDING

"A Proud New Home for the Jet Liners," *Los Angeles* Magazine, April 1961.

Heimann, Jim. "A City Lost and Found," *Los Angeles Times*, February 18, 1996.

Greenberg, Peter S. "The Best of Los Angeles: An Insiders Guide to Surviving LAX," *Los Angeles* Magazine, October 1996.

Siegmund Cuda, Heidi. "Planet LAX," *Los Angeles Times*, Feburary 6, 1997.

Hudson, Karen. *Paul R. Williams: A Legacy of Style*. New York: Rizzoli, 1993.

Hudson, Karen. *The Will and the Way*. New York: Rizzoli, 1994.

Haynes, Karima A. "The Rich Legacy of a Black Architect," *Ebony*, March 1994.

Williams, Paul R. "If I Were Young Today," *Ebony*, 1963

Gebhard, David and von Breton, Harriette. *LA in the Thirties*. Peregrine Smith, 1975.

CHAPTER 12: GETTY CENTER

Meier, Richard. *Building the Getty*. New York: Alfred A. Knopf, 1997.

Walsh, John and Gribbon, Deborah. J. Paul Getty Museum and Its Collections: A Museum for the New Century. Los Angeles: J. Paul Getty Museum, 1997.

Meier, Richard; Huxtable, Ada; Rountree, Stephen; Williams, Harold. *Making Architecture: The Getty Center*. Los Angeles: J. Paul Getty Trust, 1997.

Giovannini, Joseph. "Getty v. Guggenheim." *Art in America*, July 1998.

Weschler, Lawrence. "When Fountainheads Collide." *The New Yorker*, December 1997.

CHAPTER 13: DISNEY CONCERT HALL

Friedman, Mildred (ed.). *The Architecture of Frank Gehry*. Catalogue to the exhibition at the Walker Art Center. Works from 1964–1986. New York: Rizzoli, 1986.

Jencks, Charles (ed.) with a critical discourse by Robert Maxwell and Jeffrey Kipnis. *Frank O. Gehry: Individual Imagination and Cultural Conservatism*. London: Academy Editions, 1995.

Dal Co, Francesco and Forster, Kurt W. *Frank O. Gehry: The Complete Works*. New York: Monacelli Press, 1998.

Gill, Brendan. "An American in Paris," *The New Yorker*, Oct. 10, 1994.

Tomkins, Calvin. "The Maverick," *The New Yorker*, July 7, 1997.

Rykwert, Joseph. "An American Original," *Los Angeles Times*, May 2, 1999.

Ouroussoff, Nicolai. "In Search of Material Gain," *Los Angeles Times*, July 31, 1998.

ILLUSTRATION CREDITS

PHOTOGRAPHERS

Julius Shulman: 2, 3, 5, 8, 10, 11, 15, 16, 18 (title background), 21 (AIA office interior), 24, 26, 27 (title background), 29, 32, 43 (bottom right), 46, 60, 76, 89, 90, 91, 92

Marvin Rand: 18, 19 (lower right), 22, 23, 25, 34, 35, 36, 37, 39, 84, 85 (title background), 86 (lower left)

Tom Zimmerman: 21(lower left), 27, 77 (lower right)

Robert Millard, (Courtesy of the Los Angeles Philharmonic Archives): 41

Eric Lloyd Wright (Courtesy of the Getty Center for the History of Art and the Humanities): 48 (upper right)

The Mott Studios: 51 (title background), 57

William Eccles: 85 (lower right)

John Stephens (Courtesy of the J. Paul Getty Trust): 98

Scott Frances/Esto (Courtesy of the J. Paul Getty Trust): 99 (title background), 104

Luca Vignelli, (Courtesy of Richard Meier & Partners): 100

Jock Pottle/Esto (Courtesy of the J. Paul Getty Trust): 103

Whit Preston: 106, 109 (model shots), 112, 113

Joshua White: 107 (title background), 114

COLLECTIONS AND ARCHIVES

Tom Zimmerman Collection: 6, 52, 54, 61 (title background), 63, 67, 73–74, 86 (right)

Frank Lloyd Wright, 28 (lower left), from promotional material announcing the film, Frank Lloyd Wright by Ken Burns & Lynn Novick,

Aline Barnsdall, 28 (lower right), courtesy of the City of Los Angeles, Cultural Affairs Department, gift of David & Michael Devine

usc/Title Insurance Archives: 11 (lower right), 12, 15 (upper), 17, 30

usc/Whittington Archives: 77 (title background), 78 (lower right), 80–83

Los Angeles Public Library, Security Pacific National Bank Collection: 21 (top), 64, 78 (top and lower left),

Bison Archives: 43 (title background), 48 (lower right), 61 (lower right), 62, 69 (lower right), 70 (lower left)

Los Angeles County Museum of Art, bequest of Beulah Roth: 40

Yale University, School of Fine Arts: 58

Austin-Chalk Collection, Griffith Observatory: 68, 69 (title background), 70 (top), 71

Richard Meier & Partners: 99 (lower right)

Frank O. Gehry & Associates: 107 (lower right), 110

ACKNOWLEDGEMENTS

I would like to thank the team at Balcony Press—publisher Ann Gray, editor Danette Riddle, and designers Jim Drobka and Jim Matcuk—a collaborative group whose dedicated efforts helped create the book I envisioned. Tom Zimmerman provided invaluable assistance in locating historic material, as did the research staffs at the USC, UCLA and Santa Monica libraries. I also want to thank Frank O. Gehry for his generosity of spirit.

HISTORIC CULTURAL MONUMENT STATUS

Cultural Heritage Commission,
Los Angeles Cultural Affairs Department

MISSION SAN BERNANDO REY DE ESPAÑA
Cultural Monument #23,
Declared on August 9, 1963

BRADBURY BUILDING
Cultural Monument #12,
Declared on January 4, 1963

UNION STATION
Cultural Monument #101,
Declared on August 2, 1972

LOS ANGELES CITY HALL
Cultural Monument #150,
Declared on March 24, 1976

HOLLYHOCK HOUSE
Cultural Monument #12,
Declared on January 4, 1963

GRIFFITH OBSERVATORY
Cultural Monument #168,
Declared on November 17, 1976

GRAUMAN'S CHINESE THEATRE
Cultural Monument #55,
Declared on June 5, 1968

WATTS TOWERS
Cultural Monument #15,
Declared on March 1, 1963

CASE STUDY HOUSE #22
Cultural Monument #670,
Declared on November 9, 1999

LAX THEME BUILDING
Cultural Monument #570,
Declared on December 18, 1993